SAUDI ARABIA

By the staff of Editions Berlitz

How to use our guide

- All the **practical information**, hints and tips that you will need before and during the trip start on page 105, with a complete rundown of contents on page 108.

- The introduction on p. 6 gives an appreciation of Saudi Arabia and its people.

- For an overview of the country's **history**, both ancient and modern, consult the chapter A Brief History on page 12.

- Information on Saudi institutions and society is contained in the section **Essential Background**, p. 22.

- Saudi Arabian **cities** and **places of interest** are described between pages 36 and 91. Our own choice of sights most highly recommended is pinpointed by the Berlitz traveller symbol.

- A special section, **Arabia Deserta** (pp. 52–59), focuses on the lore of the desert, the Bedouin and the basics of desert survival.

- Spectator and participator **sports, entertainment** and **leisure activities** are reviewed between pages 92 and 98.

- Tips and suggestions on what to **shop** for are found between pages 96 and 98.

- A round-up of **local dishes**, their preparation and the etiquette that surrounds a Saudi Arabian meal are featured between pages 99 and 104.

- Finally, there's an **index** at the back of book, pp. 127–128.

Although we make every effort to ensure the accuracy of all the information in this book, changes occur incessantly. We cannot therefore take responsibility for facts, prices, addresses and circumstances in general that are constantly subject to alteration. Our guides are updated on a regular basis as we reprint, and we are always grateful to readers who let us know of any errors, changes or serious omissions they come across.

Text: Cyril Glasse
Photography: Tchekof Minosa
Layout: Doris Haldemann
We wish to thank Lindsay Morris for her invaluable help in the preparation of this guide.
Cartography: Falk-Verlag, Hamburg.

Contents

Maps

Saudi Arabia p.37; Riyadh p. 38; Jeddah p. 69; The South-West pp. 84–85

Cover photo: Riyadh Water Tower
pp. 2–3: An asphalt road crosses the Rub al Khali, linking Najran with Ash Sharura.

Saudi Arabia and its People

The Koran calls the Arabs* the "people of the middle", as if the deserts were the centre of the world. Today this seems more true than ever, as millions turn to Saudi Arabia not only for the spiritual riches of Islam, but for the material wealth of oil.

Power, prosperity and the trappings of modern technology are new to this "Desert Kingdom" with its vast tracts of barren, inhospitable terrain. The largest country in the Middle East, it covers four-fifths of the Arabian Peninsula, stretching from the Red Sea to the Gulf. Yet less than one per cent of the land is under cultivation. Rainfall is sporadic, temperatures can reach 50 °C and there is not one perennial river.

But 50 years ago the desert yielded up its secret, buried for over 500 million years in a honeycomb of porous limestone: the treasure of oil. Exploited on a large scale only since the 1960s, this "black gold" has brought unimaginable wealth to a population of less than 10 million.

Under its influence, the face of the land is rapidly changing. Massive investment in irrigation is literally making the desert bloom. Skyscraper mod-

*The term Arab is derived from a Semitic word meaning "desert". In this guide we use the word to mean the peoples of the Arabian Peninsula, although it can also be applied to their descendants in the Middle East and North Africa.

ern cities, served by futuristic airports and elevated superhighways, are mushrooming around the old mud-brick towns. Oil installations stud the desert and the inshore waters of the Gulf. Health care and education are expanding. No income tax is necessary: oil revenues pay for it all.

For most people Saudi Arabia is the land whose oil wealth is critical to the future of the world. But for 14 centuries Arabia has been revered and cherished as the birthplace of

King Fahd inaugurates a vital desalination plant.

Muhammad, founder of Islam. And for 900 million Muslims, this momentous heritage takes precedence over everything else. Every year hundreds of thousands flock to Mecca to observe the sacred rites of the Hajj (pilgrimage).

Islam is the guiding force in the life of the Saudis. The structure of government and society is based on its precepts. Islamic law, the Sharia, is observed to the letter, alcohol is forbidden, offices shut down at fixed times for prayer and life is ruled by the Islamic calendar.

With the enormous wealth generated by oil, the people of Saudi Arabia have come face to face with the problem of reconciling the values and traditions of Islam with the materialism that great riches bring. The country has become a land of opportunity with more than 2 million foreign workers, one in five of the population. Job openings attract Egyptians, Lebanese, Koreans, Pakistanis and many other nationalities, as well as large numbers of Western specialists, on whose expertise the Saudis still depend.

Nevertheless many aspects of social behaviour continue in the old tradition. The desert has moulded the character of the Arabs, and the harsh way of life of the Bedouin tribes forged the enduring values of hospitality, bravery and communal justice. Fiercely proud of their ancestry, the Saudis maintain their age-old customs in the face of rapid modernization. Like the tribal sheikhs, the king is accessible to his subjects at any time; business is concluded with ceremony; and visitors are entertained with elaborate hospitality. Even in the cities Saudi men favour a long robe and flowing head covering, because they are practical and comfortable in the extreme heat. Although the car has replaced the camel, in the desert a dwindling Bedouin population is still forever on the move in search of water and new grazing.

The Kingdom of Saudi Arabia, unified by Ibn Saud in the 1920s, consists of six distinct regions. Two of them are utter desert: the vast Rub al Khali or Empty Quarter in the south and the sandy wastes and scattered oases of the Nafud in the north. The oil-rich Eastern Province lies along the shores of the Gulf. Bordering the Red Sea coast in the west is the Hijaz, with the Holy Cities of Mecca and Medina and the

Old traditions linger as the Kingdom develops apace.

8

port of Jeddah. To the south-west extend the fertile mountain province of Asir and the Najran. And in the centre rise the mountains and plateau of the Najd, heartland of Saudi tradition, home of the royal family and site of the capital, Riyadh.

Saudi Arabia is not a conventional tourist destination. Most people come here for business or to fulfill the once-in-a-lifetime pilgrimage to Mecca. But if you have some time to spare, you should venture out and see something of this unique country. Steep ridges, rolling dunes and dazzlingly green oases contrast with the underwater wonders of the Red Sea coral reefs. You can explore the lush green vegetation of the Hijaz mountains; lose yourself in the market-place bustle of the souks; or wander out to gaze at remains of the long-lost civilizations which flourished and declined along the old spice routes.

The enjoyment and success of your trip may depend on your willingness to respect the Saudi way of life. Learn a few words of Arabic with its elaborately turned phrases— you will give infinite pleasure

The rooftops of Najran are ideal for evening relaxation.

and open the door to renowned Saudi hospitality. You may even absorb something of the Arab mentality yourself and come to believe that *qisma* or fate (our word kismet) is fixed in advance. At any rate, you cannot fail to come to terms with the key phrase *in sha allah,* meaning "God willing". It is one of the most important phrases in Arabic. Allah takes care of everything. All Saudi life revolves round this simple, but fundamental rule.

A Brief History

When the glaciers of the last Ice Age held Europe in their grip, the Arabian Peninsula was covered with lush green vegetation. As the ice retreated northwards, the sun took over, drying up the rivers and parching the soil, turning the Pen-

Vast testament to a lost civilization: a Nabatean tomb at Mada'in Salih.

insula into desert with only a fringe of fertile land to the south and west. This area became the cradle of the Arab race, which later spread from oasis to oasis across the arid interior.

The original settlers of Arabia shared a common ancestry with other Semitic peoples such as the Babylonians and Assyrians, all of whom migrated to the lands bordering the Peninsula, where they made contact with earlier populations of other races.

The Arabs emerged from the mists of antiquity with a strong sense of ethnic identity enshrined in genealogical tradition, although a distinction was drawn—and has continued to exist—between the South Arabians, who farmed the fertile, rain-favoured lands along the coast in the Yemen and the Hadhramaut (the Arabia Felix or Fertile Arabia of classical times), and the mainly nomadic North Arabians, the Bedouin tribes of the Hijaz and the Najd.

The South Arabians rose to prominence by virtue of their strategic location on the maritime routes to India and China. During the 2nd millennium B.C. they carried on a flourishing trade with the Egyptians and Babylonians in incense and spices. Frankincense, in great demand in the ancient world for temple and funeral use, and myrrh, an ingredient in cosmetic and medicinal balms, mummification and cremation, were both resins from trees found only in South Arabia.

Trade declined with the conversion of the Roman emperors to Christianity, after which the practice of cremation, and with it the use of frankincense, diminished drastically. The fall of the South Arabian hegemony was signalled decisively by the collapse, through neglect, of the famous Marib dam in the Yemen in 580.

Meanwhile, around 500 B.C., a North Arabian tribe had established the Nabatean Kingdom, centred on Petra (in present-day Jordan). For over 400 years Petra was the key city on the caravan route between Sinai and the Mediterranean, but in A.D. 105 the Romans absorbed the Nabatean territory into their empire.

The nomadic Bedouin tribes in the hinterland of the Arabian Peninsula remained in virtual isolation, although Christianity and Judaism reached a few tribes. The Hijaz boasted only three cities: Ta'if, and the sister cities of Mecca and Medina, of which Mecca was then a centre of pilgrimage for the pagan tribes of the desert. The history of the Bedouin before conversion to Islam in the 7th century A.D. was mainly a tale of guerrilla wars based on territorial disputes and blood feuds between tribes which were recorded in legend and poetry.

The Beginnings of Islam

The period leading up to the mission of Muhammad is known as the *Jahiliyah* (Period of Ignorance). The religion of Abraham was preserved by the Christians and Jews and some Arabs, but many Arab tribes worshipped pagan idols installed in the sanctuary of the Ka'aba in Mecca. This, then, was the Arabia into which Muhammad was born to breathe fresh life into the Peninsula. He swept the idols out of the Ka'aba in favour of the one God, Allah, united Arabia as never before, and through the Bedouin tribes, spread its influence under the banner of Islam far beyond its confines. (For life of Muhammad, see p. 31.)

Muhammad was succeeded by Abu Bakr (632-4), the first of the four so-called patriarchal caliphs. While most of the Bedouin tribes had sworn allegiance to Muhammad, they were less willing to comply with his successors. However, Abu Bakr soon reunited the Peninsula, and the Arabs were ready for the first stage in their expansion.

The justification for conquest was the concept of *jihad* (holy war) which demanded that idolatry be wiped out, but the reason was also economic: to find a source of income to replace trade, which had been disrupted during Muhammad's war against the Meccans (see p. 32). This was achieved by raiding neighbouring territories, an age-old Bedouin practice, and carrying back booty and supplies to sustain the impoverished Muslim community. Remarkably the two great powers of the time, the Christian Byzantines and Sassanid Persians, whose empires bordered on the Peninsula, crumbled under the onslaught, and the Arabs found themselves surging forward into Syria and Iraq. Damascus fell to the Arabs in 635, while a separate force in Iraq took the Persian capital, Ctesiphon. By 642 the Arabs had wrested Egypt from Byzantine hands.

The Umayyad dynasty, with its capital at Damascus, presided over the second phase of Arab conquest, during which the territories of the Islamic

Empire reached their greatest extent, stretching from the Bay of Biscay to the Indus and the confines of China, and from the lower cataracts of the Nile to the Aral Sea.

Within a century of the death of Muhammad, his followers had succeeded in creating an empire unrivalled in the world at the time. But, with the fall of the Umayyads in 750, the truly Arab phase in the history of the Islamic Empire passed. Although the Abbasids (750–1258), ruling from Baghdad, witnessed the golden age of Islamic civilization, the great accomplishments in art, medicine and philosophy, the building of great mosques and observatories, and the discoveries of science were largely achieved outside the Peninsula. But the Arabs had made their unique contribution—an inspiring religion and language which provided the unifying force.

The Peninsula itself fragmented into petty sheikhdoms. The Hijaz was ruled by Sharifan families, descendants of the Prophet, while the desert tribes ruled themselves by consensus through their elected or hereditary sheikhs. The pilgrimage to Mecca was the basis of the economy for the coastal areas, and camel breeding for the interior. The shifting of power in the outside world was reflected by the acknowledgement of suzerainty by the major Arabian cities, in turn, to the Fatimids of Egypt, the Ayyubids of Damascus and, finally, from the 15th century on, to the Turks of Istanbul.

The Rise of the House of Saud

The modern history of Saudi Arabia begins in 1744 when the chief of a clan north of Riyadh, Muhammad ibn Saud, Sheikh of Dir'iyah, made an alliance with a puritanical religious leader, Muhammad ibn Abdul Wahhab. They pledged to purge Arabia of deviations from orthodox Islamic beliefs and to initiate a period of spiritual and moral reform. This union of temporal power and religious authority formed the basis of a system of government which endures to this day.

Ibn Abdul Wahhab and his followers, *muwahiddun* or "unitarians", had a stringent definition of *shirk,* the attribution of divine qualities to anyone but God (for instance, the veneration of saints), and were opposed to *bi'dah,* innovations not sanctioned by the Prophet.

By the terms of the pact, the House of Saud undertook to support the Wahhabi movement—even with the sword if **15**

The Arab Steed

Tradition says the Arab horse sprang from five mares owned by King Solomon 3,000 years ago. Descendant of the wild Kuhaylan and ancestor of the Thoroughbred, it is noted for its intelligence, beauty, speed and stamina. Its characteristics include a fine small head with flaring nostrils, compact short back, silky mane and high-set tail. The predominant colour is the grey or white of the romantic image of the Arabian horseman.

The horse was developed in early times in Arabia by intensive inbreeding and excelled in battle. By the 3rd century, a stock had been introduced into England where, in the 17th century, the Arab was combined with other breeds to produce the Thoroughbred. The first Arab horse reached North America in 1765.

"After woman came the horse, for the enjoyment and happiness of man." So said the Prophet Muhammad, who is believed to have owned 15 mares in his lifetime. Today, the tradition of fine breeding continues in stud farms in the Najd region of Saudi Arabia and is fostered by a keen interest in racing and by the eagerness of foreign buyers.

the need for *jihad* arose. Which indeed it did, for many were the opponents of the new doctrine. But the zeal of the Wahhabis prevailed. Riyadh, Dir'iyah's closest neighbour, was taken in 1773, and soon after the turn of the century, much of the Peninsula, including the Holy Cities of Mecca and Medina, had fallen into their hands. One campaign even reached the outskirts of Damascus.

The Ottoman authorities in southern Iraq were so alarmed by the proximity of this threat that the sultan ordered his governor in Egypt, Muhammad Ali Pasha, to crush the movement. Muhammad Ali's son, Ibrahim Pasha, laid siege to the capital Dir'iyah in 1818 and razed the city to the ground. Abdullah, great grandson of Muhammad ibn Saud, was executed in Istanbul and other members of the family scattered in defeat. It seemed that the new Arabia had been destroyed forever.

But the Wahhabis again rallied round the representative of their dynasty, Abdullah's

Above: The National Guard on parade. Below: "There is no god but God; and Muhammad is His Prophet"—eternal words inscribed on the Saudi flag.

cousin Turki, who had escaped at Dir'iyah. He established himself in Riyadh in 1822 and founded a new state. His assassination in 1834 and ensuing family squabbles over succession paved the way for their rivals, the Turkish-backed Rashid, who had made their base at Ha'il, to seize Riyadh in 1891. But, Turki's great grandson, Abdul Aziz ibn Abdul Rahman as Saud, later to be known as Ibn Saud, escaped to wreak vengeance. He was smuggled out of Riyadh in a saddle bag on his father's camel at the age of 12 and grew to maturity in exile in Kuwait.

In the autumn of 1901, Ibn Saud set out with 40 warriors to restore the family fortunes. This was to prove one of the most spectacular raids of modern history, with all the classic ingredients of stealth, surprise attack and near defeat turned into victory.

It was a cold winter in the desert at the end of the month of Ramadan. After the feast of Id al Fitr following the fast, Ibn Saud and his companions reached the walled city of Riyadh. Using a palm tree as a ladder, they scaled the wall and gained access to a house opposite the Musmak Fortress, where they waited until dawn. When the Rashidi governor

was leaving the fort to return to his private house, they charged at him. As he attempted to climb back through the heavy door, a spear thrown at him missed and stuck in the doorpost. The spearhead remains to this day. The governor ducked back through the door, but was overpowered and killed. With the fort in his hands, Ibn Saud soon became the new ruler of Riyadh, and the supremacy of the House of Saud was reasserted.

The young victor introduced a number of measures to gain the support of the tribes and to establish a more stable society, in which the foundations of law and order were based on the Koran. A new social and economic framework was to replace the nomadic way of life of the Bedouin. Settlements of *ikhwan* (brethren) were established in agricultural communities, the first of which was at Artawiya in northern Najd. These settlements also served as sources of manpower, ready to fight to the death for the Wahhabi cause.

Ibn Saud became known as the Emir of Najd, seriously challenging the ambitious Sharif Hussain of Mecca. In 1913 he took Hufuf, capital of Al Hasa, from the Turks, who had remained his principal rivals.

Birth of a Nation

Ibn Saud and Britain had a common goal in World War I in the defeat of the Turks, and relations were established through Britain's agent in Kuwait, Captain Shakespear, one of several diplomatic figures to be captivated by Arabia and by the personality of Ibn Saud. Shakespear, in full combat uniform despite the desert heat, joined Saudi troops and lost his life at the hands of the Rashid at the Battle of Jarrab in 1915.

Arab nationalism was fostered by another Englishman, T.E. Lawrence, who won the name "Lawrence of Arabia" by helping to liberate the western part of the Peninsula from Turkish domination through attacks on the Hijaz railway.

After World War I, when Faisal, son of Sharif Hussain of Mecca, became King of Iraq and offered his support to the Rashid family, it became even more important for Ibn Saud to capture the rival stronghold of Ha'il. This he did in 1921, and then he liberated the Holy Cities from the rule of the Sharif. In 1926 he was proclaimed King of the Hijaz as well as of the Najd in the Great Mosque of Mecca.

An Islamic congress was immediately convened to discuss administration of the sanctuaries at Mecca and Medina, to ensure that the Holy Cities would be accessible to the whole of Islam and would not become Wahhabi preserves. This, along with exposure to a more cosmopolitan world in Jeddah, upset the *ikhwan* extremists and forced Ibn Saud to overpower these dissidents at the Battle of Sibilla in 1929. In 1932 the union of Najd, Hijaz, Asir and Al Hasa was officially named the Kingdom of Saudi Arabia.

The Fountain of Wealth

With the country united, Ibn Saud granted a 60-year concession in 1933 to Standard Oil of California (SOCAL) to prospect for oil, following its discovery in neighbouring Bahrain. Eight American geologists sailed from Bahrain to explore a dome-shaped hill called Jabal Dhahran. With few maps available, the area had to be explored by aerial photography. Equipment was landed in 1935 and the first well drilled. By the end of 1937 the number of Americans had increased to 50 and six more wells had been sunk—all without success.

At that time Ibn Saud was more interested in water than oil. He invited geologists to Riyadh to drill artesian wells. Two of the experts, on their day off, went to the famous waterhole of Ayn Hit. As they approached the bottom of the path leading to the pool, they identified the same cap rock formation found in Bahrain, evidence that oil must be trapped underneath. With this information, it was decided to deepen the seventh of the abortive wells in Jabal Dhahran. In March 1938, oil was struck at 1,550 metres, nearly a mile below the surface of the hill.

With the outbreak of World War II, operations were suspended, but they resumed in 1944 and the Arabian American Oil Company (ARAMCO) was formed. The subsequent history of Saudi Arabia is inextricably bound up with the story of oil and the phenomenal wealth and influence it has brought.

The last 20 years of Ibn Saud's life saw a period of consolidation at home and greater participation in world affairs. Saudi Arabia featured as one of the founder members of the United Nations and the Arab League. When Ibn Saud died in Ta'if in 1953, covered with 42 battle scars, he had become a legend in his own time, a figure that seemed to have stepped out of the past and walked into the 20th century, bringing a new nation with him out of the cobwebs of obscure desert feuds. In accordance with Wahhabi tradition, he was buried in an unmarked grave.

The new kingdom had been created not only by the sword,

A haze of heat blurs the view of an east coast refinery.

but also by marriage links between the Saud family and other desert tribes, engendering loyalty and a guaranteed succession. Ibn Saud left 43 sons and many more daughters. He was succeeded by his eldest son, Saud, who instituted a regular ministerial system and a National Planning Council. But, by the end of the 1950s, the economy was failing and it fell to his brother Faisal to introduce a series of reforms. In 1964, with civil war brewing in neighbouring Yemen, the *ulama* (a body of religious scholars) and other princes persuaded Saud to abdicate in favour of Faisal.

A deeply religious man,

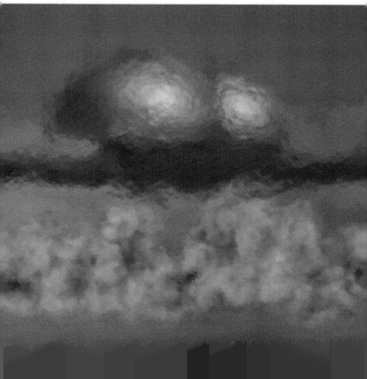

Faisal was also a pragmatist who saw the necessity for technological advancement. In his view there was no incompatibility between the rigorous tenets of Islam and the material and scientific progress made possible by the oil boom.

With this in mind he laid down the enlightened goals for the first and second development plans which included education for girls, training of Saudi personnel, improved housing and health care and a sound infrastructure. His profound commitment to Arab solidarity against Zionism led to the oil embargo of 1973 in protest against Western support of Israel. In 1975, seated at a traditional *majlis,* Faisal was shot by a deranged nephew.

The succession passed smoothly to his brother Khalid, also a moderate man, who continued to steer the country towards rapid social and economic change. He died in 1982 and was succeeded by yet another brother, King Fahd.

During the 20th century, the House of Saud has established itself as one of the most influential ruling families in the world, unifying a country of feuding tribes and giving its name to a kingdom of extraordinary wealth and striking contrasts.

Essential Background

Government

Saudi Arabia is an Islamic monarchy, but autocratic rule is moderated by a system which takes into account the views of the tribes grouped round their hereditary sheikhs, the religious leaders in the *ulama* and members of the widespread royal family. Under the laws of succession, brothers take precedence over sons, so that Ibn Saud's successors until now have been his sons.

The king is prime minister, as well as the Imam, leader in prayer and religious matters. He turns for advice to a Council of Ministers, many of whom are members of the royal family. The royal family also acts as a consultative body which, through its own network, relays the people's grievances to relatives in the government. All important decisions are based on a consensus of opinion. There are no political parties in Saudi Arabia.

There is no formal constitution. Guidance for both ruler and citizen is based on God's law, the Sharia, drawn from the Koran. The Sharia, meaning the "path to follow", is a comprehensive system of ethics, morality and religious duties dealing with civil and criminal matters. It is implemented by the *ulama* and by religious courts, whose judges *(qadi)* are appointed by the *ulama*. The defendant may have a lawyer, but it is the *qadi* who weighs up the evidence, acting both as judge and jury. The accused is innocent until proved guilty. Penalties are harsh and meted out in public. Murderers may be beheaded if the relatives of the victim demand it. This prevents long-standing feuds between families.

The death sentence is also customary for adultery, though the act must be proved by the testimony of four eye-witnesses.

The idea that all men are equal before God is exemplified in the practice of the *majlis,* whereby the king is accessible to the people at regular intervals to hear their petitions.

Several of the king's brothers hold top ministerial posts, including HRH Crown Prince Abdullah ibn Abdul Aziz, First Deputy Premier, and HRH Prince Sultan ibn Abdul Aziz, Minister for Defence and Aviation.

Prince Abdullah, brother of King Fahd, is next in line to the throne.

The Economy

Oil has made Saudi Arabia one of the wealthiest nations in the world, but fluctuations on the international oil market during the last decade and a possible **23** limit of 50 years on reserves have prompted a flexible development strategy. The government has been anxious to diversify the sources of national income by founding competitive industries and providing incentives to the private sector.

The Third Development Plan (1980–1985) is designed to steer the Kingdom towards industries such as mining, construction and consumer-product manufacture, so as to increase exports and promote self-sufficiency by training a Saudi workforce to replace foreign expertise. The Saudi Industrial Development Fund backs new businesses in which foreign investors are still encouraged to participate, while new laws regulating the operations of foreign companies protect Saudi contractors. Petrodollars, oil revenues invested abroad, are now being ploughed back into the economy. The Saudi Consultancy House publishes the results of market research studies and the Ministry of Industry is setting up permanent exhibitions of national products in Riyadh Industrial Town.

A sound infrastructure is also being created through expansion of service industries, such as electricity and telecommunications, and the building of roads, schools, housing and hospitals has continued at an astonishing pace. New airports at Jeddah and Riyadh have been designed to cope with the increase in passenger and cargo traffic.

Oil. Saudi Arabia is the world's largest exporter of oil and also has the largest reserves. The country is second only to the Soviet Union in terms of oil production, which amounted to 6 million barrels a day in 1983.

The 14 main oilfields are situated in the Eastern Province and in the Gulf. Safaniyah is the world's largest offshore oil-

A Barrel of Oil

There's really no such thing. This measurement convention arose in West Virginia in the U.S. in 1866 as a means of standardizing the haphazard practice whereby buyers brought their own barrels to cart away oil from the pump. Naturally capacity varied, so the producers decided to sell by the gallon. They reckoned an average barrel at 40 gallons and threw in an extra two for good measure. But the name barrel stuck, so that even today production is estimated in "barrels" of 42 gallons. In some countries oil is also measured by the metric ton, equal to 7.2 U.S. barrels.

field and Ghawar the largest onshore field. Increased domestic demand is leading to the construction of new oil refineries.

Petromin is the state-owned organization responsible for the development, exploitation and marketing of oil, mineral and natural gas resources. It operates the famous Petroline, the crude oil pipeline which runs for 1,200 kilometres from the oilfields in the Eastern Province to the Red Sea coast, linking the industrial cities of Jubayl and Yanbu. Petromin refineries cater for the domestic as well as the export market. All other industrial develop-

ment is administered by the Ministry of Industry.

Natural gas is the second major source of revenue and the Master Gas System constitutes the backbone of long-term industrial development. Gas flares were once a feature of the landscape, but this valuable source of energy is now being used as fuel for local industry and feedstock for petrochemical plants, as well as to produce propane, butane and natural gas for export. Gas

A Saudi workforce keeps abreast of the new technology.

Threshing is still done by hand in the Asir. Heavy machinery does not suit the mountainous terrain.

has also played a vital part in the development of the electric power system of the Eastern Province.

Minerals. Apart from oil, the Kingdom's mineral resources include copper, gold, zinc and extensive iron ore deposits.

Water is a precious commodity in short supply. Waste water and sewage is recycled for irrigation. Desalination is literally in the pipeline with the "Saudi superpipe" which carries treated seawater from Jubayl on the east coast to Riyadh. This stretch of 470 kilometres breaks the record for the longest continuous welded water pipe. Desalination plants are being installed by numerous foreign companies.

This is only one of many projects aimed at generating

cultural output, even though only a tiny proportion of the land is under cultivation. Through substantial interest-free loans and subsidies to farmers, the government aims to make the country self-sufficient in foodstuffs. It is already self-supporting in vegetables and fruit, and the yields of wheat, barley, maize and alfalfa are increasing yearly. The highest output has come mainly from the Asir region in the south-west, which has the greatest rainfall.

Experimental farms in the Eastern Province are a thriving business. The biggest dairy farm in the Middle East lies here in the Al Kharj region, and sheep are reared on irrigated pasture on the edge of the Empty Quarter. Poultry farming is gaining popularity. It is hoped that the provision of basic transport and communications, together with health and educational facilities in rural areas, will continue to stem the tide of migration to urban areas.

supplies of the country's scarcest resource. With an average rainfall of less than 100 millimetres a year in most areas except the south-west, water must also be sought underground. Engineers are drilling wells, installing water pumps and building dams and reservoirs. A sound investment: "I would not exchange it—even for an oilfield", says one well-owner near Jubayl.

Agriculture. Increased water supplies have improved agri-

Fishing. The fishing industry has grown substantially in the Red Sea and the Gulf. Eighty per cent of the catch is destined for home consumption. Top-quality shrimp are exported, especially to the United States and Japan.

27

Islam

"There is no god but God; and Muhammad is His Prophet." Everywhere you go in Saudi Arabia you will see and hear these words; they are even inscribed on the national flag. The affirmation of the formula is called the Shahada and represents the basic tenet of Islam, the religion of the Saudis and of one in five of the world's population.

The word *islam* means "submission", acceptance of the will of Allah, the one true God. Muslims believe that Muhammad was divinely chosen in the 7th century A.D. to make known to the world God's final message, the essence of which had been previously revealed to prophets such as Abraham, Moses and Jesus.

God's words, as spoken to Muhammad by the Angel Gabriel, were noted down on stones and palm leaves or preserved in the memory of the Prophet's disciples. After Muhammad's death, the revelation was compiled in written form in the Koran, the chief source of Islamic doctrine. The Koran is considered by Muslims to have incomparably beautiful language, so that if it were translated into another language, it would no longer be the Koran. Therefore, whatever the mother tongue of the Muslim, the Koran is quoted everywhere in Arabic and every educated Muslim is familiar with the Arabic script. Islam accepts the Torah, the Psalms and the Gospels of Christianity, as interpreted by Muslims, to be also divinely revealed.

In the world of Islam there is no distinction between a secular life and a religious one. The Koran is the single, indisputable power which unites Muslims around the world and extends its control over every aspect of life. Whenever the Koran gives no direct answer or is silent on a particular point, the deeds and sayings of the Prophet (Sunna), as fixed in the Hadith (Traditions), are looked to for guidance. The Koran and Sunna regulate the basic and recurrent facts of everyday life,

Friday is the day for congregational prayer.

The Five Pillars of the Faith

Muslims see their faith as a road with five signposts or pillars along the way. If the believer performs these duties, he will be assured of a place in paradise.

- The Shahada or profession of faith is the affirmation: "There is no god but God; and Muhammad is His Prophet."
- Prayers *(salat)* must be said while facing Mecca five times a day: at dawn, at midday, in the latter part of the afternoon, at sunset and at nightfall. These times are proclaimed from the minarets of mosques by the muezzin (criers). After ritual ablutions, prayers take from five to ten minutes, involving sacred recitations and culminating in a prostration, with the forehead touching the ground. The midday prayer on Friday is a congregational prayer and all men are expected to go to the mosque.
- Almsgiving includes a compulsory religious tithe *(zakat)* payable to the poor, as well as voluntary donations to the needy or gifts for a mosque.
- Fasting is required of Muslims during Ramadan (the ninth of the twelve lunar months), in which the Koran was revealed. From sunrise till sunset, strict abstinence is observed in all matters, including food and drink. A cannon is fired to signal the beginning and end of each day's fast. Those who are ill or travelling are exempt, but must make up the fast whenever they can. The end of Ramadan is celebrated by the feast of Id al Fitr.
- The Hajj, or pilgrimage to the Ka'aba, Islam's most sacred shrine, should be undertaken once in a lifetime by all who have the means and the health to make the journey.

---

such as the way to greet each other, the way to wash and the way to eat.

The Muslim house of worship is the mosque, which not only serves the spiritual needs of the community, but also acts as a meeting place and a centre for religious instruction. Traditional features of the mosque are the *mihrab* (prayer niche) placed to indicate the direction of Mecca, and next to it, the *minbar* (pulpit). Islam allows no priests or elaborate ceremonial, but the *imam* (guide) leads the prayers in the mosque, and a body of religious scholars, the *ulama,* takes decisions on matters whose solutions are not found in the Koran or Sunna.

Early in the history of Islam, during the caliphate of the last of the four orthodox caliphs, a schism occurred out of which Shiism emerged. Shiism is a sect of Islam which believes in an inspired leader who inherits a right to spiritual and temporal dominion by virtue of his descent from the Prophet. Except for a small Shiite minority in the Eastern Province, Saudi Arabia is overwhelmingly Sunni, or orthodox.

Life of Muhammad
Long before Muhammad, Mecca was already a holy place. It was believed that after expulsion from the Garden of Eden, Adam and Eve were reunited on the Mount of Mercy beside the Plain of Arafat.

By tradition, the original Ka'aba was built by Adam, although it was Abraham who reconstructed it and established a pilgrimage to it.

The story of Abraham's absolute obedience to God is central to the message of the Koran. (Arabs regard Abraham as their progenitor and trace their descent from his elder son Ismael, while the Hebrews trace their line from the younger son Isaac.) It tells how Abraham's childless wife Sarah gave her maid Hagar to her husband, how Hagar bore Ismael, and how the jealous Sarah drove Hagar out into the desert where mother and child were only saved by a miraculous spring of fresh water welling up from the sand at Zamzam.

Abraham returned some years later to find Ismael and together they rebuilt the Ka'aba, around which Hagar and Ismael were to be buried.

A town, Mecca, grew up around this shrine and flourished as a mercantile centre on the trade route from South Arabia to the markets of the Levant. It also became a centre of idolatrous worship—until God's revelation to Muhammad heralded the new era of Islam.

Muhammad was born around A.D. 570 into a highly respected family of the leading Quraysh tribe in Mecca, but was orphaned as a small boy. At the age of 25, he married a rich widow, Khadijah, and under her aegis prospered as a merchant. In A.D. 610, while on a meditative retreat in the mountains near the city, he had a vision of the Angel Gabriel telling him to "recite in the name of the Lord ... who teacheth man what he knows **31** not". The revelation took the form of *surat* or verses describing man's relationship to his Creator, Allah.

The Prophet returned to the city and told his wife and family of what had happened. They were among his first converts. However, when he began preaching in public, he met with instant hostility. As the new teaching began to gain ground among all classes of society, the merchants of Mecca, in particular the powerful Umayyad clan, one of the most prominent in the whole Quraysh tribe, became alarmed, seeing the new religion as a threat to Mecca's status as a sanctuary and centre of pilgrimage. Numerous attempts were made to silence Muhammad and his followers.

Soon it became apparent that even his life might be in danger, so Muhammad sought asylum with a neighbouring city, Medina, where there were already a number of Jewish tribes. The emigration, or Hijrah, of Muhammad and his followers to Medina in A.D. 622 marks the starting point of the Islamic calendar. At the time, Medina was embroiled in bitter tribal feuds. The inhabitants welcomed Muhammad as an independent arbitrator and many converted to his creed.

With the Medinans behind him, Muhammad began a war of attrition against Mecca, by harassing their caravans and thus their livelihood. A full-scale conflict ensued, with the Medinans emerging the victors against heavy odds. After seven years of exile, Muhammad returned to Mecca in triumph. The Prophet destroyed the idols in the Ka'aba and rededicated it to the one God of Abraham.

Before he died in A.D. 632 Muhammad had established a form of government for the new religious community. He had also created ties with the surrounding nomadic tribes, who converted to Islam.

Today, Islam has spread to all parts of the globe, but it has preserved its essentially Arab spirit, a nomad sense of space and a union with a centre— Mecca.

Adapting to Saudi Society

Many customs in Saudi Arabia are undergoing rapid change. Because of outside influences, certain modes of behaviour are no longer so rigidly maintained. However, it is as well to familiarize yourself with the etiquette and traditions. You will appreciate the people more if you understand how they think

and act, and in return they will appreciate your courtesy and consideration.

The family is the all-important social unit. Though Saudis are entitled to four wives, many nowadays have only one. Arranged marriages are still common. Never ask after a Saudi's wife. They may, however, ask after yours, because they know that it is acceptable to do so in the West. The extended family system is very much in operation, and rela-

The coffee ceremony can be a family affair or a rite of hospitality.

tives remain in close touch with each other.

Saudi women still live in relative seclusion. A woman leaving the immediate family circle will be veiled and must not be alone with a man other than her husband or a close relative. Traditionally men and women do not mix in public, but in some circles they are now invited to dine together. Women still generally eat separately from their menfolk and in some households female guests will be treated likewise. Women are not allowed to drive cars in Saudi Arabia.

Complete strangers will often be very hospitable and may receive you like an old friend. Courtesy demands a similar attitude in return. To avoid the embarrassment of having to say no to someone, or to engage in delicate negotiations, the use of a third party may be very useful. Symbolism matters: never sit so that the soles of your feet are directed at anyone. Don't beckon with your index finger. Speech should be decorous. Sobriety of manner is considered a desirable trait; laughter should be subdued, never raucous. Men should not wear shorts except at the beach. Women should keep their knees and elbows covered. Western women often wear a long black cape or *abaya* over their clothes when going out into the street. Remove your shoes before stepping on a carpet.

Shaking hands at meeting and parting is very important; Arabs often kiss on both cheeks (or make the gesture from a distance) when meeting a friend. When accepted, you too could be greeted in this way. Saudi men can often be seen holding hands in comradely affection. Otherwise in most circumstances keeping a certain distance is the rule in the Peninsula.

If you drop by to see someone, be prepared to stay for tea or coffee, and perhaps a snack. When receiving people, offer refreshments, even if you are in a hotel. There are certain formalities of precedence when invited to tea or coffee in somebody's house, though these are not always strictly observed. As a guest you may be offered the first cup, which you should return to your host with the words *sharrif,* "do me the honour", or *ishrab,* "drink". The offer will be declined and the cup returned. Then you may drink. It is the custom to drink three cups of coffee, but the cups are usually tiny. Give your cup a twist or shake when returning it, to signify that you have had enough.

There is always a moment of polite hesitation before starting to eat. Ancient Arab custom established that noble actions are performed with the right hand and ignoble ones with the left. It is always better to use the right hand to take and to give, and if eating with one's fingers, to eat with the right hand only (the etiquette is to use the thumb and first two fingers daintily). Conversation usually takes place before and after the meal and it is always advisable to ask permission before being the first to light a cigarette. After the meal, coffee will be served and incense passed around. This is the final rite of hospitality and a signal for people to leave.

In business, visitors are often received with many others present. It is not a sign of disrespect to have one's own business treated in series with that of others. It reflects the practice of the *majlis,* or sitting together for discussions in the sheikh's tent, and the essentially egalitarian nature of Arab society. Allow time for pleasantries and the serving of tea or coffee before commencing business. Don't show impatience. "Haste comes from the devil" is an old Arab proverb. Remember that business is interrupted for prayer.

When seeing high government officials it is important to wear a suit and a tie, at least until a personal acquaintance is built up. When looking for a gift for a Saudi business associate, often a man who has everything, you can never go wrong by giving masculine varieties of eau-de-cologne. These are used all the time and are one of the things Saudis carry in their ubiquitous briefcases. It's a good idea to carry business cards printed in Arabic, as well as English.

When the time for prayer is called by the muezzin, people pray wherever it is clean and convenient. Never walk immediately in front of someone who is praying; if possible leave at least a few metres distance. Non-Muslims should not attempt to enter a mosque which is a consecrated place for prayer. Above all, non-Muslims are completely banned from the sacred precincts *(haram)* of Mecca and Medina. During Ramadan even non-Muslims must not eat, drink or smoke in public or in the presence of Muslims during the daylight hours.

Photography is a sensitive subject. Don't take photographs of women, mosques or military establishments without permission.

Generosity may dictate that an admired object should be presented to the admirer, but a certain non-covetous admiration for things like falcons and horses, points of pride for their owner, is not misplaced.

On the whole, smoking is looked down upon and it is better to refrain (especially women) until the preferences of your companions are known. **35**

Where to Go

There is more to Saudi Arabia than cities and desert and, with good communications by air and road, many of the remoter regions are now accessible. You can enjoy the beaches and marine life of the Red Sea, the contrast of sand and oasis, or the mountain greenery of the South-West. Numerous archaeological sites shed light on the Arabia before Islam, but permission must be obtained to visit them. Inevitably your first port of call will be one of the big cities: Jeddah, on the Red Sea coast, or the capital, Riyadh.

Central Province

The great plateau of the Najd, "the Highlands", lies at the heart of Saudi Arabia. Bounded by the two desert expanses of the Nafud and the Rub al Khali, it is made up of shallow vales, steep ridges, mountains sometimes rising to 500 metres, and river beds long since run dry. Nomadism remains a traditional though disappearing feature of the region, and oasis settlements have fostered a thriving agriculture. One such village was Riyadh, now the fast-expanding royal capital.

Riyadh

Soon after arriving in Riyadh, it dawns upon the visitor that this great modern city is really only a small island floating in a vast ocean. From the mountains of the Hadhramaut in the south of the Peninsula all the way to Damascus, from coast to coast: desert. Not necessarily sandy, like the Nafud or the Rub al Khali, but desert nonetheless. This sense of emptiness pervades Riyadh through its non-existent city limits as it does all the cities of the Najd.

This is the Wahhabi homeland, purposeful, strict, God-fearing. There is no street life with loungers in the evening as in Mediterranean cities. The older houses are all mute fortresses, and the new ones, more often than not, have walls which peer unblinkingly at all the passers-by, with no indulgence for the idle stroller. The sun beats down with an astonishing intensity (although winters can be cold). But the city still has, in its austerity, a certain elegance that only desert towns possess: they blend into their surroundings, and so take on some of the majesty of the landscape.

Riyadh is a city spreading its wings. Not so long ago it was closed to outsiders, even though it was the capital, ac-

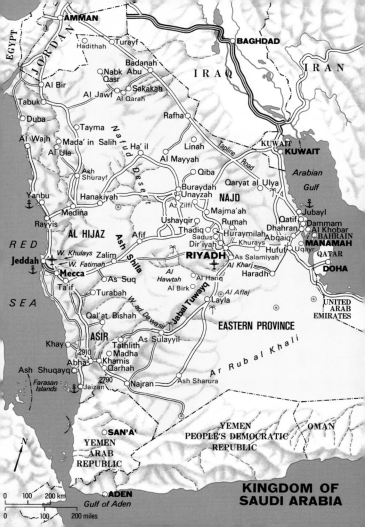

KINGDOM OF SAUDI ARABIA

Attalah House

Defence and Aviation

British Council

Obeid Hospital

Malaz Park

Intercontinental

King Faisal
Conference Centre

Interior

Riyadh
Palace

Faculty of Arts

University of Riyadh

Al Murabba

Communications

US Information
Service and Library

Agriculture
and Water
Resources

Industry and
Electricity

Mövenpick

Al Jami Mosque

Education

Vocational
Training Centre

Health

Al Bourge Building
(Round Tower)

Commerce

United Nations
Development
Programme

Finance and
National Economy

Visas and
Passports

Pilgrimages and Waqfs

Language
Institute

Public Works
and Housing

Shara Al (Al Yamamah)

Shara Umar Ibn Al Khattah

Bab Al Nasiriyah

Fish Suq

Shara Al Imam Abu Hanifah

Stores Publisher's
Residence

Post Office

Al Malik
Abdul
Aziz Mosque

Qasr Al
Murabba

Royal Technical
Institute

Shara Al Malik Saud Bin Abdul Aziz

Qasr Nura

El Khreigi

General Post Office

Library

Al Tai

Water Tower

Qasr Al Hamra

Riyadh

Salam

Hadikat
Al Futtah
Park

Al Haramain

Al Hamra

Museum
of Archaeology
and Ethnography

Al Nasr

Shara Al Imam Faysal Bin Turki

Al
Rawdhah

Al Jazirah Bank

Cairo

Al Quds

Suq Batha

Kuwait Suq

Traditional
Najd House

Saudia Office

Al Marqab Mosque

Traditional
Najd House

Citibank N. A.

(Al Shemaisi
Jadeed)

Qasr al Adl

Jami (Friday)
Mosque

Al Musmak Fortress

Suq

Bin Marbub Mosque

Dira Square

Telephone and
Telex

Qasr al Hukm (Emirate)

Ibn Atiq Mosque

Traditional
Najd House

Al Khaimah

Salman Mosque

(Sibalah)

Shara Khalid Bin Al Walid

RIYADH

MECCA, JEDDAH

Mosques

Ministries

Hotels

Markets (suq),
Stores

General (Palaces,
Banks, Historic
Landmarks)

500 m

500 yard

cepting them only by special dispensation. Now it has at last opened its doors to the foreign embassies which will move from Jeddah.

Riyadh, the "Gardens", originated as a series of settlements which sprang up around the luxuriant date palms of the Wadi Hanifah. At the turn of the century, the city covered a comparatively small area, but now the old mud-brick buildings and slender minarets are overshadowed by towering office blocks. Evidence of the fundamentalist form of Islam espoused by the House of Saud can be seen alongside luxury imported goods, smart shops, American cars and modern development schemes. Wide tree-lined streets accommodate the increasing traffic and over a million inhabitants. Maps are almost instantly out of date.

Al Matar Street, the road from the airport, is lined with imposing government ministries and hotels. Look out for the **Ministry of Petroleum** which is a fine example of traditional architecture adapted to modern times, and **Qasr al Murabba,** the famous cubic palace built in 1936 for King Abdul Aziz ibn Saud, founder of the Kingdom of Saudi Arabia. The king, in the traditional manner, was accessible to any of his subjects wishing to submit a personal petition. The cool, dark *majlis* (reception hall) saw a steady stream of visitors. The palace of Princess Nura, Ibn Saud's favourite sister, is nearby.

The elegant striped **Water Tower** is the central landmark and symbol of the city's dependence on deep wells. The welcome greenery of the **Hadikat al Futtah** park nearby offers pleasant surroundings for a rest. The **Qasr al Hamra** palace, built in 1953 by King Saud, now houses the Council of Ministers.

Old Riyadh

The Riyadh of the 1930s encompassed the Adl, Hazm, Salam, the southern part of the Washm and the Hillat al Abid districts. The latter means the slaves' quarters but, since slavery was abolished in 1961, it is sometimes called the "Quarters of the Emancipated". To conjure up a picture of what the city was like, it is worth taking a leisurely stroll through the area.

Some older-style Najdi buildings still stand, particularly near Mecca Road (Tariq Mecca al-Mukarramah). The crenellations are of a distinctive style; often there are loopholes rather than the luxury of windows. **39**

Palm trunks, yet another service this generous tree renders to the dwellers of the desert, were used as the inside building supports, particularly for the arcades around inner courtyards. Bands of various decorative patterns, the most typical of which are leaf shapes in a wheelspoke arrangement, were impressed into the wet clay. The doors provided the builders with a chance for exuberance: painted decoration, studs and other ornamental designs are the only splash of sumptuousness in the midst of otherwise great sobriety. The walls slope inwards at the top and, together with the squarish proportions, give a sense of resistance and austerity.

The no-man's land between the houses used to be patrolled by *mutawiyyin,* religious vigilantes armed with sticks on the lookout for laxity, non-observance and sin. The *mutawiyya,* or "inducer of obedience", is an institution peculiar to Wahhabism, enforcing strict conformity to the law in a sector which is elsewhere left to conscience. Today they are particularly active in the markets, sometimes riding in cars with loudspeakers, making sure that shops close for prayer promptly after the muezzin's call.

40   At the heart of the old

town, just off Thumairi Street, rises the impressive mud-brick **Musmak Fortress,** symbol of the emergence of Saudi Arabia from Turkish domination. Here was enacted the scene of Ibn Saud's daring raid in 1902 (see p. 18). The point of a spear aimed at the governor can still be seen in the massive

wooden door. The fortress is being restored as a museum.

On nearby Dira Square, you will see the **Qasr al Adl** (Palace of Justice) and the **Qasr al Hukm** (the Emirate Government Palace), where the king holds regular meetings with tribal sheikhs and the *ulama*. The square can act as a public

Symbol of the city, Riyadh's Water Tower is an eye-catching landmark.

execution ground. On one side stands the **Great Mosque,** also known as the Jami or Friday Mosque, built on the site where Emir Turki ibn Abdullah was assassinated in 1834.

41

The Souks

There's no better way of getting a taste of an Arabian city than by strolling through its souks. A visit to the **Bedouin Souk** or antique market, in a warren of alleys off Uthman ibn Affan Street, is like discovering treasure trove. Here you can lose yourself among stalls selling daggers, incense-burners, Turkish-style coffee pots, copper-studded Zanzibar chests, embroidered bags, suits of armour, muskets and wooden well wheels.

All that glitters is gold at this stall in Riyadh's Gold Souk.

The **Tent Souk** *(Suq al Khaimah),* near Dira Square, has canvas work and Bedouin weaving.

The **Batha Souk,** on the corner of Al Khazzam and Al Batha streets, sells everything from cardamoms to cameras. You may also find jewellery worked by local craftsmen.

Always an entertaining outing is the **Camel Market** *(Suq al Jamal),* where you can watch the aristocratic beasts standing patiently by, eyeing the whole proceedings with disdain.

In the **Pottery Souk,** off Wazir Street, you'll find all sorts of locally made handicrafts, including the *narguilah* or water-

pipe and unusual musical instruments.

At the **Women's Market** *(Suq al Harim),* behind Dira Square, you will be offered filigree silver jewellery and other Bedouin handicrafts.

Also behind Dira Square is the **Gold Souk,** where gold jewellery is valued by the gram. Prices vary from day to day according to the world gold prices, but they still represent considerable bargains in comparison to Europe or the United States.

Modern Riyadh

Most of the urban development has sprung up to the north and west of the old town, while the residential areas lie to the east. **Malaz Park** offers welcome shade, and the racecourse nearby is open during the cooler months. The **Zoo,** with its entrance off Al Ahsa Street (also known as Zoo Road), boasts a variety of exotic animals, as well as native oryx, gazelle and baboons.

Jabal al Mahruq, near the stadium, is worth a visit. The natural rock formation which forms a bridge at one spot was a favourite haunt of Ibn Saud, who used to come out of Riyadh and sit in its shade and gaze out over the city. Called by some the "Eye of the Needle", it is now known as Camel's Eye Park.

Saudi Arabia's first museum and one of its major attractions is the **Museum of Archaeology and Ethnography,** on Imam Abdul Aziz ibn Muhammad Street. It contains a splendid collection of treasures, a record of the many civilizations that have blossomed in the Arabian Peninsula through the millennia. Besides the artefacts, arranged in a clear and attractive way with explanations in depth, there is a multi-screen, audio-visual presentation of the country's history. The largest gallery, called "After the Revelation", provides an introduction to Islam. In the museum garden is a display centred on a black, goat's-hair Bedouin tent. The results of major excavations are on view. The Department of Antiquities and Museums in the same building will give you information on archaeological sites worth visiting. Permits to visit these may be needed.

The **Folklore Museum** in Riyadh University's College of Arts building offers a fascinating introduction to those aspects of Saudi life that a foreigner has little or no opportunity to witness. The collection includes writing boards on **43** which pupils used to learn the Koran, regional clothing, falconry implements, pottery and musical instruments. Everyday artefacts no longer in use will give you an idea of what to look out for in the souks.

Members of the Saudi royal family live in palaces on the road to Dir'iyah in the direction of the Olympic Sports City and the new university. In contrast to the older buildings, there are some distinctive modern ones—the **Riyadh Conference Palace** and the **King Faisal Conference Centre.** The ultra-modern hospital, which also bears King Faisal's name, is a little further out. The various departments of King Saud University are moving to a prestigious site on the outskirts of the city. The centrepiece of the new campus is the King Khalid Eye Hospital.

Riyadh's dry healthy climate makes a pleasant change from the humidity of the coast and, for weekend excursions, there is some spectacular scenery to be found quite close to the city: dramatic escarpments of sand, fertile wadis (dry river beds), and flat plains dotted with acacia, leading to verdant date groves. In this arid setting, you can observe unexpected plant and animal life and fall asleep under the stars.

South of Riyadh

A favourite spot for weekend outings is **Ayn Hit,** a natural waterhole 50 kilometres south of Riyadh on the Al Kharj road. The spring attracts bathers to its warm, clear water over 30 metres down in a giant cave. It is thought to be part of an underground river flowing through the Al Kharj region and on into the Gulf. Ibn Saud is said to have stopped here to water his camels before his raid on Riyadh in 1902 (see p. 18). And when oil prospectors had become discouraged, the discovery here in 1937 of a type of rock which causes oil to accumulate beneath it gave new impetus to explorations and led to the first strike at Dhahran.

Al Kharj, about 100 kilometres south of Riyadh, has been developed for agriculture, thanks to a massive irrigation scheme started in the 1930s. The wadis, fed by underground springs, create lush gardens with groves of resplendent date palms—a perfect place for a picnic.

Continuing south, you get further away from the urban tumult of the 20th century and ever closer to the life of the desert nomad. A good road runs from As SALAMIYAH to **Layla,** a large agricultural village named after the heroine of a Bedouin love story, in which a young man wanders the desert crying for his lost love. The village was a stronghold of the *ikhwan,* the crusading warriors of Ibn Saud who carried the Wahhabi reformation across Saudi Arabia.

The surrounding region, Al Aflaj, gets its name from underground water cisterns, possibly of Persian origin. Some are still in use. Servicing holes are dug and channels burrowed to connect the holes. The channels operate on a slight slope so that water can travel from a remote source to the villages. Not far from Layla a treat awaits: Saudi Arabia's only two **natural lakes.** Birds and butterflies take advantage of this delightful spot, along with campers, boaters and water-skiers.

From Layla the road continues to As SULAYYIL, a good starting-point for a trip into the desert.

A new road, linking up with Najran, passes through one of the Kingdom's richest archaeological sites at **Qaryat al Fau.** In the late second and first millennium B.C. it became a prosperous city on an ancient trade route between the spice-producing areas in the south and the ports of the Gulf. Evidence suggests it was also an important wheat-growing area

and may have been the capital of the legendary kingdom of Kinda. Recent finds include wall-paintings and bronze statues. Excavation continues under the auspices of King Saud University in Riyadh.

A turnoff from the As Salamiyah–Layla road takes you down **Wadi Hawtah** through a succession of villages nestling among clusters of date palms and fruit trees. Drive on to AL HARIQ, through a typical oasis which ends abruptly at the foot of the dramatic **Tuwayq Mountains,** which extend for 650 kilometres from the Nafud desert in the north to the Yemen border in the south. Rough tracks cross the range and join up with the main Riyadh-Jeddah road, but this is only for the adventurous.

Another approach to the Tuwayq escarpment is from the Jeddah road about 30 kilometres from Riyadh. Through a gap in the ridge, you will see some red sand dunes called **Irq Rathimah,** a superb campsite under sheer cliffs of sand. A track through the sand dunes will lead you to an ancient burial site. In the bottom of a wadi stand some strangely shaped stones, remnants of some mysterious cult. The escarpment is capped by limestone deposited by ancient seas **45** which once covered the area, so you may be lucky enough to find shell fossils 150 million years old.

Two camel trails climb the Tuwayq escarpment. These constituted the original trade routes from Yemen to the Gulf and were also used by pilgrims on their way to Mecca.

The mud ruins of Dir'iyah have been preserved as a national heritage.

North of Riyadh

Dir'iyah, the old walled capital of Saudi Arabia, lies 18 kilometres north of Riyadh on an escarpment overlooking the date groves and fruit trees of Wadi Hanifah. It was here that the alliance was struck between Muhammad ibn Saud and the religious reformer Muhammad ibn Abdul Wahhab (see p. 15). The pact sparked off a struggle that, through moments of victory and crushing defeat, was to last into the beginning of the

20th century, when the Hijaz and the Najd were finally united by Ibn Saud.

Most of the old mud buildings are in ruins following bombardment by a Turkish-backed Egyptian army in 1818. From the heights of Dir'iyah you look down into the wadi through which they dragged their heavy artillery to the citadel of Turayf, where the Saud family made their last stand. Across the wadi rise the watchtowers which guarded the approach.

The mud ruins of Dir'iyah stand silent, untouched. They are safe from the city planners and the steam shovels because they are the visible, tangible genealogy of the Saudi state and nation. Restoration is now being undertaken by the Department of Antiquities and Museums in Riyadh.

Sadus, a picturesque oasis about 20 kilometres further on, with date palms and dusty streets preserves the atmosphere of old Arabia. The 300-year-old fortifications include a round tower and a dominating fortress. The mosque, with winter and summer prayer-halls, is a fine example of local architecture. Permission to visit the mosque may be obtained from the local Emir.

Huraymila, further north on the main road to Majma'ah, is, by contrast, a modern town, though there are some remains of Ottoman walls and palaces built by Ibrahim Pasha during his invasion of the Najd. The wadi beyond is an attractive camping spot. South-west of town lies the starting-point of the old Mecca road used by pilgrims and traders for centuries.

Still further north, the Sudayr region makes a rewarding trip. The well-preserved oasis towns and desert dunescapes are typical of the heartland of

Arabia. The main road to Majma'ah by-passes a number of small towns enclosed within solid walls. **Majma'ah** has many modern facilities but retains a characteristic old town dominated by a fort. Beyond Az Zilfi, the sand dunes are a natural form of architecture, changing colour in the sunlight from orange to glaring white. After the spring rains, they are covered by a brief magic carpet of wild flowers.

Buraydah, the principal town of Qassim province, can be reached from Az Zilfi, crossing the scorching desert. It has always been an important trading crossroads and is today the site of some comprehensive farming experiments: cattle and sheep farms and a new agricultural institute. Irrigation channels have transformed the arid landscape; orange and lemon groves, vines, pomegranates and bananas flourish alongside marrows and tomatoes. But this Garden of Eden soon gives way to hundreds of kilometres of stony desert which stretch all the way to Medina. The main attraction in the town is the old central square where you will find a cool, covered souk and a group of watermelon sellers beside the mosque.

The perfect region for a week-end excursion stretches northeast of Riyadh, where several wadis lie between the Tuwayq Mountains and the Dahna Sands. **Wadi al Jafi** is on the old Bedouin route to the wells on the edge of the Dahna Sands. Here you can survey your surroundings from the shade of acacia trees, or look

for fossilized sea-urchins in the chalky hills round about.

RUMAH is the last refuelling post on the old Riyadh-Kuwait road before you head across the **Dahna Sands.** The sands run from the Nafud desert in the north to the Empty Quarter in the south with dunes sometimes rising to an awesome 75 metres.

For the intrepid, there is always the Darb Buwayb, a track starting 20 kilometres out of Riyadh on the Khurays-Dammam road. The sand dunes to the west of the track, **Irq**

This lush oasis in the desert is no mirage.

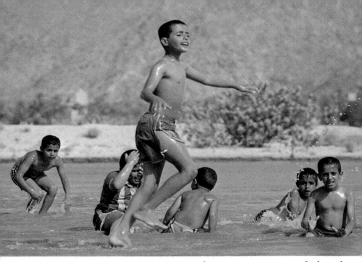

Rain fills a dry wadi—to the delight of local children.

Banban, are covered with wild flowers in the spring. Two natural waterholes and grazing for goats and camels attract Bedouin encampments to the area.

The Far North

Ancient cities of Arabia once flourished in the north of the Peninsula: Al Jawf (the Biblical Dumah) and the towns of the Wadi Sirhan. The inhabitants were linked, if only by conquest, to the kings of Assyria, Babylon and Persia, and the monuments and inscriptions on the rock formations show the influence of these civilizations.

Ha'il, in the province of the same name, is situated on a fertile plain between the black mountains of Jabal Shammar and Jabal Salma. It has its own airport for domestic flights but can also be reached by road from Buraydah and Riyadh.

Just as Dir'iyah tells the story of the House of Saud, so Ha'il was once the capital of their illustrious rivals, the Rashid (see p. 18). They controlled the area as far north as Al Jawf until Ibn Saud came to power and unified the country. His capture of the town is recorded in one of two impressive forts.

Standing at the crossroads of four major trade routes, Ha'il was once a town of some importance, but few of the old buildings are left. The remains of the **Rashid palace** are worth seeing for the superb mosque with its decorated walls and beams of whole palm logs. You'll need a Muslim guide.

The souk sells rugs, pottery and other crafts. The black, goat's-hair tents of the Bedouin, a reminder of the proximity of the Nafud desert and the austere life of the nomad, can be seen on the outskirts of the city.

Al Jawf, an oasis town, lies at the most northerly point of the vast empty wastes of the Nafud. The name Al Jawf means a geographical depression, indicating the position of the old town on the slopes of a great basin with steep cliffs around. Protected from the endless red dunes, the palm groves, orchards and fields of grazing cows conjure up a pastoral scene.

The **Qasr Marid,** a magnificent fortress, dates back to the 2nd century B.C., and a little further north is the 7th-century **Mosque of Umar** with its 20-metre-high minaret. The town is also noted for the camel races held at the Islamic New Year.

Flights from Riyadh, Jeddah and other cities land at nearby **Sakakah,** another oasis town, 50 kilometres north-east of Al Jawf, and of importance as the seat of the local Emir or governor. The regional museum houses early pottery and carved stone figures.

At the bottom of the mud fort by the side of **Jabal Burnus,** you'll find some fascinating pre-Islamic drawings of dancing girls.

Mysterious life-size stone figures can be seen some 15 kilometres to the south near AL QARAH. Known as the **Rijal al Hajar** (Men of Stone), these curious sculptures tell the story of a Bedouin tribe punished for irreverence by being turned to stone. For this expedition you need a four-wheel-drive vehicle and a guide.

The Wadi Sirhan, stretching north-west of Al Jawf, has always been a strategic route between Syria and northern Arabia and has given rise to a group of oasis settlements known as **Qarrayat al Milh** (Villages of Salt). The village of ITHRA claims the most important ruin, a **Nabatean Palace** dating from the 1st century B.C. Also worth seeing is the **Rwallah fort** near the village of UGAYLAH. Domestic flights go to TURAYF or AL HADITHAH. **51**

Arabia Deserta

Saudi Arabia's two great sand deserts, the Nafud and the Rub al Khali, are like vast expanses of water; few settlements break up these oceans of shifting sand. The Rub al Khali is known to foreigners as the Empty Quarter, but the Arabs call it simply "the Sands". Stretching over an area of 654,000 square kilometres in the south of the Peninsula, the Rub al Khali is the world's largest continuous body of sand, bigger than the whole of France. The Nafud in the north covers 57,000 square kilometres.

Though huge, these deserts are far from monotonous. The colours are vivid and vary from deep orange in the early morning to creamy white at midday. The Nafud has a warm red hue, caused by the iron oxide in the sand, to which the grey-green tamarisk bushes are a welcome contrast. For the really dramatic sandscapes, you must venture far away from the urban centres. Although this is now made easier by an expanding network of good roads, some tracks are still only suitable for four-wheel-drive

52 *Spring rains bring life to the desert.*

vehicles—or there is always the camel, to give you the real feel of desert travel.

The sand often builds up into dunes, sometimes reaching a height of over 300 metres. Dunes are formed by sand particles blown into piles by the wind or collected round some obstacle. They slope gently up on the windward side and then drop steeply. The shapes of the dunes constitute a form of living sculpture in constant state of evolution. Where the wind is constant, a whole dune may gradually be moved forward—sometimes as much as 30 metres a year. The ancient city of Gerrha (present-day Uqayr) may well have been engulfed by moving dunes and, more recently, parts of the Al Hasa oasis were saved in the nick of time by the planting of millions of tamarisk trees to act as wind breaks.

Plant life is surprisingly varied and perfectly adapted to desert conditions. Some seeds lie dormant for years and only spring to life as if by magic after a sudden rainfall. After the spring rains, the desert may acquire a green sheen caused by the sprouting of minute plants often decked with exquisite tiny flowers.

Some animals have also come to terms with the harsh environment. Many are nocturnal, most are sandy-gold for camouflage. Lizards, hares and foxes still abound, but the larger species, including the oryx, ostrich and gazelle, have become virtually extinct as a result of indiscriminate hunting, which is now illegal.

The Desert Nomads
The Bedouin are the traditional hardy inhabitants of the desert, and many travellers have had cause to be grateful for their in-

Bedouin extend the hospitality of the desert.

54

stinctive knowledge of the terrain. They still make up about 15 per cent of the Saudi population, although increasing numbers have been lured away by the comforts of city life.

The Bedouin are proud of their history and traditions, and many aspects of their way of life endure to this day in Saudi Arabia, even in the settled communities. Hospitality was considered an absolute duty, and protection was granted for up to three days to anyone who sought sanctuary with a tribe—even a declared enemy. The mutual obligations incurred through "sharing salt" were often invoked by the British traveller Charles Doughty when hostile strangers had to be reminded of the bond of nourishment shared. "Tightening the belt" is another expression which probably originated with the Bedouin. Forced to live at subsistence level, they would often tighten their belts of plaited leather to still the pangs of hunger.

Equality was an essential ingredient of Bedouin life, and the tribal sheikh, chosen for his wisdom and qualities of leadership, would always arbitrate, never dictate. This patriarchal tradition is still seen at the Saudi king's weekly *majlis,* when anyone can bring a

request or complaint and call his chief "brother".

The Bedouin cultivated the art of falconry, the breeding of fine horses and camels. They also raised the saluki, a hunting dog whose purebred nature exempted it from the usual religious abhorrence of dogs, normally considered unclean.

Another feature of Bedouin life used to be the *razzia* or raid, carried out mostly against travellers or different tribes. It was a proof of manhood and served as a means of acquiring posses-

A waterhole is a welcome sight in the arid wastes of the Rub al Khali.

sions, though these would often be reclaimed by the plundered tribe. Blood feuds could last for generations. With the introduction of firearms and motorized transport the mortality rate rose dramatically. Raids were finally outlawed by Ibn Saud, who also encouraged the tribes to settle in sedentary, law-abiding agricultural communities.

The life of the Bedouin was hard, simple, noble and poetic. But modern times are catching up with them and forcing them out of their black tents and into cinderblock housing, off their "ships of the desert" and into Toyota trucks. If you see them, salute them graciously, this might be the last generation.

Desert Survival

The desert may be a refuge from the fast-moving, hard-living 20th century, but it is also a very different world, with a code of conduct which you must respect in order to survive. There is a harsh reality to the romance, so be prepared:

Route. Inform someone of your intentions—the names of those travelling, the route planned and the anticipated duration. Plan in detail before setting off. Stick to what is feasible within the time. Allow for regular stops along the way and don't try to cover more

Ship of the Desert

The camel of Arabia, the one-humped dromedary, excels as a riding and pack animal over vast desert distances. Even today, it is more reliable than the trucks which are displacing it and is indispensable to the Bedouin.

Camels can go for days without water; their spreading, padded toes tread the soft ground without sinking; and they can subsist on coarse grass and thorny bushes, storing fat in their hump against hard times. The driver can tell from the hump how much energy is left; if the camel is driven too hard, the hump shrinks. But when the camel finally reaches water it can drink up to 100 litres at a time to regain its lost weight in a few minutes.

To keep out sand, camels have two rows of eyelashes and can close up their nostrils. They run with a rhythmic pacing gait which is said to have influenced the lilt of Arabic poetry.

Apart from transport, these versatile animals provide meat, milk, and cloth woven from their coarse hair for shelter and clothing. Even their dung can be burned on cold desert nights. And at the end their skin provides leather for belts, waterskins and saddles.

than 250–300 kilometres in a day. Avoid travelling at night. If lost or stranded, always stay with the vehicle.

Vehicle. Four-wheel drive is essential. You'll need to carry extra oil and petrol, as well as spares in case of breakdown: two wheels, a jump lead, fan belt and tow ropes. For good measure throw in spark plugs, a hand pump, a fire extinguisher and a couple of spades.

Documents. Don't set off without your passport, driving licence, car registration papers, insurance and residence permit.

Essentials. You'll need a compass and adequate maps. Bedding should include sleeping bags, blankets and a tarpaulin, which can also be used to get the car out if it gets stuck in the sand.

Clothing. Wear loose, light cotton clothing and cover your head. In winter, take something warm; the nights can be chilly. Wear desert boots; snakes, although rarely encountered, are extremely poisonous, and sandals provide little protection. Shake out your shoes before putting them on as scorpions can also be a hazard. And don't forget your sunglasses.

Health. The main danger is heat stroke. This occurs when the body loses too much moisture and salt through perspiration. Symptoms are nausea, vomiting, dizziness and weakness. Take salt tablets dissolved in water and wear a hat. Try to avoid the midday heat. Also essential to your first aid kit are aspirin, water-purifying tablets, diarrhoea pills, insect repellent, disinfectant, bandages and, of course, sun cream. It is best not to take young children or elderly people on expeditions into the desert.

Water. You should drink 6 or more litres of liquids a day, so carry a good supply of water with you. And remember that even in the dryest desert it is possible to gather small amounts of water by improvising a solar still to catch condensation. For this you need to dig a small pit and drape a sheet of plastic over it, weighed if necessary by a small stone so that its lowest point hangs directly over a cup placed in the bottom of the pit. The sun's heat will draw any moisture from the soil, which will condense on the *underside* of the plastic and drip into the cup. This could just be enough to save a life.

Desert transport: the truck may be more comfortable, but the camel is still more reliable.

Eastern Province

The Eastern Province is today synonymous with oil. Indeed it holds the largest oilfield in the world, the Ghawar, which accounts for much of the oil that Saudi Arabia produces. But not so long ago this province was known by its other name, Al Hasa ("The Wells"), and was renowned instead for its giant oasis with over a million and a half palm trees.

The area claims to be the original homeland of Abraham. Archaeological evidence indicates that Eastern Arabia played a vital role in cross-cultural contacts during the third millennium B.C. due to its far-flung trading operations.

Major Greek trading centres existed on the Gulf at Thaj, Hinna and Gerrha and a necropolis has been excavated at Jawan. Under the Ottoman Empire, the area formed part of a province which stretched as far as Baghdad. In 1913,

when Ibn Saud ousted the Turks with the support of Bedouin tribesmen, he gained possession of a piece of land which must now be the most valuable on earth.

Long before oil, Al Hasa's wealth was based on the date palm and the sea. Uqayr was its port, and the oasis of Hufuf generated most of the trade. Today Hufuf is the centre of a rich agricultural area, thanks to a vast underground water table. An irrigation scheme with

3,000 kilometres of concrete channels distributes water from more than 60 artesian springs to remote areas. The region has always been famous for its succulent *khalas* dates, but it now produces wheat, rice, figs, peaches, citrus fruits and all kinds of vegetables. The Hufuf branch of King Faisal University specializes in agronomy.

Oil Towns

A fantastic web is spun around Dhahran: thousands upon thousands of kilometres of pipeline bristling with forests of "Christmas trees", the clusters of valves that suddenly spring up out of the ground in the middle of nowhere. The pipelines link pumping stations in over 40 oilfields with the refinery in Ras Tanura (one of the four largest in the world) and the tank farms where the oil is loaded onto tankers bound for Europe, America and Japan.

ARAMCO's impressive activities engage 40,000 employees in the Eastern Province alone. Of these only about 4,000 are American, while 18,000 are Saudi. Armies of engineers, technicians and workmen maintain oil production,

Pipelines transfer oil from refinery to supertanker.

while drillers fly off to camps in the vast Empty Quarter to explore for new wells.

Only a few decades ago, the triangle of Dhahran, Al Khobar and Dammam offered nothing but desert and a few grazing camels. Now it is a huge, sprawling city stretching as far as Jubayl, 85 kilometres up the coast. The whole region spells OIL.

Dhahran ("Promontory") is the centre of the oil empire, the site of the ARAMCO administrative headquarters. Living quarters are extensive, but there is nevertheless a squeeze for space, which has caused the mushrooming of a number of provisional camps for bachelors. Women are allowed to drive within the compounds.

Despite the relatively small number of American employees, a distinctly American flavour pervades the area, with Parent-Teacher associations, U.S. Boy Scout Patrols and even Greyhound buses. Recreational facilities abound—a golf course, bowling alleys, cinemas and recreation centres.

The **University of Petroleum and Minerals,** dominating the area from the top of a hill, is a much noted example of modern architecture, boasting long beige-coloured arcades, fountains and a high water tower.

At night, thanks to its brilliant illumination, it becomes a point of orientation, visible from a great distance. Within the university is a mosque, large conference hall and an extensive specialized library. The **Oil Exhibit Centre,** near the East Gate of the town, traces the industry's development.

Another architectural centrepiece is the **Dhahran Air Terminal** designed by the Japanese-American architect Minoru Yamasaki. Its exuberant, golden, upward-sweeping arches have become world famous. As plans proceed for a new and larger airport, the future of this landmark remains to be determined.

Al Khobar used to be the port for Dhahran, but it has been superseded by Dammam. It is nonetheless a boom town boasting a variety of good restaurants, chic boutiques and supermarkets. Most expatriate personnel are housed here.

Dammam is the administrative capital of the Eastern Province and home of the petroleum branch of King Faisal University. Like Al Khobar, Dammam is laid out in a rectangular grid pattern and, while it does not have the same cosmopolitan sophistication as its sister cities, the market is more animated and there is a large gold souk and a sector where traditional items can be found. During the Hajj season, pilgrims from Iran, Iraq and Afghanistan trade in their carpets here to finance the journey to Mecca.

Trips to Gulf islands such as Jurayd and Bahrain can be made from Al Khobar or Dammam. Dhows, the traditional Arabian sailing boats, leave the piers early in the morning.

Jubayl, chosen as the centre of a colossal development pro-gramme, is a new industrial city. It began as a peaceful fishing village, but the harbour has now been expanded to facilitate export of Saudi Arabia's massive hydrocarbon resources. There are refineries, petrochemical and fertilizer plants, a steel mill and many other service industries. The 14-storey control tower of the commercial port is an outstanding landmark. There is also a vast desalination plant which pipes thousands of litres of fresh water a day as far as Riyadh. The Berri Natural Gas Liquids Centre has set the pace for the country's entire gas-gathering programme.

Modern, yes; but Dhahran University blends beautifully with its surroundings.

Oasis Towns

These are a different world from the oil boom towns, and their history goes back to the dawn of time. When the Portuguese under Albuquerque harried the Gulf in 1507, they were already late-comers, almost the last of many invaders. They built a fortress on Tarut Island off Qatif, taking advantage of a prominence that is probably the remains of structures dating from the 3rd millennium B.C. Ceramic fragments from the Ubaid period (5,000 B.C.) demonstrate links with the ancient Mesopotamian civilizations.

In the past, Qatif and Hufuf often provided refuge to religious minorities. The radical and contentious sect of the Qarmatians, who stole the black stone from the Ka'aba in 930, kept it hidden in Hufuf. It was returned after an absence of 20 years. Even today the tradition of religious nonconformity persists and much of the population of the oasis is Shiite.

Hufuf means "Whistling of the Wind" because in June the *shamaal* or north wind can raise spectacular dust storms here. There are two ancient mosques and a fortress, **Qasr Ibrahim**, where the Turks took refuge in 1913 during Ibn Saud's siege of the city. The **Khizam Palace**

is another handsome fortress. Don't miss the early morning **camel market** on Thursdays. At the entrance, women sell balls of newly spun camel and sheep wool.

The **Hufuf Souk** has the greatest variety of traditional and modern handicrafts in the Eastern Province. You may

Thanks to irrigation, cereal crops thrive in desert conditions.

even find some ancient chain mail armour, helmets or other antiques here. The women have their own souk, where they offer handsome wool saddle-bags, small rugs, beads and pieces of Bedouin jewellery. Look out for the striking *murassal* or silver chains decorated with balls and coloured glass or semi-precious stones that are looped, several at a time, around the crown of the head to hang down on either side of the face. If you're hungry after **65**

The Arabian Staff of Life

Among the oldest of cultivated plants, the date palm has been grown in Arabia for 4,000 years and may well have originated there. It needs less water than any other food crop, grows to 30 metres and will bear fruit for two centuries. A single tree yields up to 100 kilos of dates.

Because they are highly nutritious—54 per cent sugar and 7 per cent protein – dates have always been a staple food in Arabia. A century ago, nearly 70 varieties were grown, with names such as "Mother of Perfume" or "The Bride's Finger". Today, the most common variety is the *ruzaiz* and the best is called *khalas*. A palm cultivator must climb the tree at least four times a year, to clean, pollinate, and support branches and to cut down clusters of dates at harvesting.

Saudi Arabia has 7–9 million date palms—10 per cent of the world's total—just about one for every member of the population. Every part of the tree is used: poor quality dates and pits for fodder, the leaves for mats and baskets and the wood for building and cooking. Even the shade serves to protect wheat crops and fruit gardens.

all this shopping, try the whole-wheat bread—it's a speciality.

Worth visiting about 10 kilometres east of Hufuf is a strange pink rock formation, the **Jabal al Qarah.** This is a mountain seemingly riddled with cracks that run up and down through it. You can enter the network of caverns and wander for great distances. Don't go too far without precautions, because you could get lost. Opposite the caves, there is a settlement of potters whose vases and jars of the distinctive local colour make pretty and inexpensive souvenirs.

Qatif, another lush oasis town, is on the coast 15 kilometres north of Dammam. The Qarmations made a naval base here, and traces of their fortifications still remain. Today its port is too shallow to be of much use and Qatif is more remarkable as an oasis.

Many old houses still stand, with decoratively carved doors, overhanging balconies and wind towers to catch the breeze and circulate it through the house. Thursday is market day. Local straw-weavers sell baskets made of palm leaves in natural-dye colours and beyond, in a large courtyard, you'll be greeted by the noisy exchange of parrots in the bird market. The souk in the centre of town has a wide choice of imported goods. Nearby, Bedouin women sell carpets with a local striped design.

Characteristic of the oasis area are the white donkeys which at one time were an important export. You may see them at work, carrying building materials, often lavishly decorated with henna designs.

Tarut, an island just off the coast of the Qatif oasis, is regarded by archaeologists as the oldest known town site in Saudi Arabia. It was one of the main centres of the Sumerian civilization which flourished in southern Mesopotamia 5,000 years ago. The city became well-

known as a market for pearls, lapis lazuli and other precious stones. Tarut connected the mainland with ancient centres of civilization in present-day Pakistan, Egypt and Iran. The huge burial mound, crowned by the ruins of a **Portuguese fort,** has revealed links with the ancient Sumerian culture of Dilmun, relics of which were also found in Bahrain. Access to the fort is forbidden to men, as the local women bathe and do their washing here.

It takes skill and care to fashion a Hufuf pot.

The island's port, **Da-rin**, makes a pleasant picnic spot. One of the most recent layers of history can be seen here in what remains of a Turkish fort built in 1875. Today **Qasr ad Darin** peacefully faces an emerald sea, the last of its cannon half-buried in the sand.

A causeway now links Tarut to the mainland and, where the road comes to a dead end in Qatif, there is a domed Turkish bath-house near some date groves.

Jawan, 10 kilometres south of Ras Tanura, is a field of sandy hillocks, where a 2,000-year-old tomb complex is said to have been built for a wealthy local chief and his family. It was uncovered by an ARAMCO bulldozer in 1952. The finds here include bronze ornaments, gold jewellery and some alabaster goddess figures. They can be seen at the Museum of Archaeology and Ethnography in Riyadh.

Uqayr may be the site of the lost city of Gerrha, which became a fabulously wealthy trading post on the spice route. It was once Al Hasa's chief port. Mud wall ruins surround a fort where camels used to be loaded with sugar, coffee and copper to be traded in for dates and other oasis produce at Hufuf.

Western Province

In the Hijaz, diversity is the key word. Arid, stony desert, a steaming coastal plain, cool mountain tops and a coral paradise are all facets of this Western Province bordering the Red Sea. The human landscape is as varied as the natural. Nomads walk side by side with townspeople, farmers do business with merchants, and pilgrims from all over the world add another dimension, turning the cities of the Hijaz into a microcosm of the Islamic world.

The name Hijaz means "barrier", and refers to the great escarpment that runs parallel to the Red Sea, dividing it from the plateaus of the interior. Between the escarpment and the sea stretches the great Tihamah plain, which long ago served as a corridor for the spice caravans on their way to the rich markets of the Fertile Crescent. Two small trading centres that sprang up along this route are now the two holiest cities of Islam—Mecca and Medina. Some 88 kilometres from Mecca lies Ta'if, whose delightful situation and pleasant climate have made it the summer retreat of the king and government. Jeddah is the main city of the region.

JEDDAH

N

| | 0 | 500 m |
| | 0 | 500 yards |

Mosques
Ministries
Hotels
Markets (suq), Stores
General (Palaces, Banks, Historic Landmarks)

AL HAMRA SQUARE
Al Malik
King Abdul Aziz International Airport
Agriculture and Water Resources
Justice
Defence and Aviation
Sorour Al Sabban
Shara Muhammad
Abu Zinadah
Caravan Shopping Centre
Shara Al
New Taj
Petroleum and Mineral Resources
Shara Ash Sharafiya
Hospital
Police Station
Finance and Nat. Economy
Kaki
Kandara Palace
Education
Post Office
Al Attas Oasis
Airport
Al Badr Sheraton
Labour and Social Affairs
Baghdadiya Rest House
Saudia Headquarters
Foreign Affairs
Police Station
Al Manaqabah Lagoon
Castle Barracks Palace
Shopping Centre
Al-Malik Abdul
Municipal Office
Asia
Old Customs House
Al Rehala
Bahauddin
Atlas
Shara Al Sahifa
Khayyam
Al Fallah
Suq al Badu
Tariq - Mecca
Salam Meridien
Communications
Royal
Al Ma'mar
Tariq
Former British Legation
Suq
Bait Nassif
Mecca
Health
Queen's
Traditional Ottoman Residence
General Post Office
Building
General Hospital
Al Eid
Arab Bank
Cairo Bank
Abu Shawat
Khuzam Palace Gate
Redec Centre
Sharia Court
Khuzam Palace
Shara Al Amir Fahd
Al Amarat
Vegetable Market
Al Halabi
Islamic Development Bank
Information
Chamber of Commerce
Port Fire Station
Customs House
Shara Al Malik Faysal
Petroleum and Mineral Resources
Post Office
Sabban Stadium

RED

SEA

Jeddah

You can't help but be caught up by the excitement of Jeddah. Perhaps nowhere else in the world do so many nationalities rub shoulders in such a strangely familiar way. For centuries, as a port for the Holy City of Mecca, Jeddah has been the crossroads of the world. Now as the principal shipping centre for the Kingdom, the city keeps its cosmopolitan air.

A legend that Eve was buried here accounts for the name, which means "Grandmother". Known also as the "Bride of the Red Sea", Jeddah was officially established as the gateway to Mecca in A.D. 646 by the Caliph Uthman and continued to attract pilgrims, many of whom settled. The Portuguese built the city walls early in the 16th century, but it was the Ottoman Turks who retained uninterrupted domination until 1916.

For those entering the Kingdom for the first time through Jeddah, the port city may come as something of a surprise. As far as the eye can see there are tall, new buildings and other futuristic structures bursting through their scaffoldings towards the sky. Elevated highways loom out of vast worksites hidden in forests of construction cranes and swerve off around geodesic domes, new shopping centres, and mushrooming housing projects.

As a result, maps have to be constantly revised and municipal geographical notions brought up to date. New roads are planned to cut across and around the city and even bridge

the lagoon and harbour. Already, as new streets appear and others vanish, their names change and finding your way around may be a problem. Many streets are popularly known not by their official names but by landmarks.

The approach road to Jeddah is lined with whitewashed

Jeddah enjoys a spectacular waterside setting.

apartment buildings, factories and millions of trees and shrubs, which have already helped to cool the torrid Red Sea climate along this coastal strip of the Hijaz region. **71**

Jeddah boasts the world's longest **Corniche** and Saudi families drive their cars right down to the beach. The road runs along the sea front and sweeps round to the port. On rare occasions, you may see flocks of pink flamingoes matching the sunset.

As summertime relief from the oppressive humidity, make for the **Bahr al Ahmar,** a popular waterside park benefiting from cool offshore breezes.

Jeddah youngsters grow up in a city of contrasts.

The **Al Hamra quarter,** facing the Red Sea and the Corniche Road, is the most elegant neighbourhood. The large, handsome royal guest palace which is situated here has attracted around it many more palaces and fashionable residences, as well as chic shopping centres, stores and restaurants.

The Old Town
Al Alawi Street runs through the heart of the old town. At night, the nearby side streets are lit with old-fashioned lamps and, during Ramadan, food stands spring up selling juices, salads and tasty snacks.

Look out for the **Ma'mar**

Masjid (Mason's Mosque), one of Jeddah's oldest monuments, dating from the 16th century. Most celebrated of all are the **merchants' houses,** four or five storeys high, made of coral rock quarried in the Red Sea. As this rock was calciferous and soft, the houses were not very durable and those standing today were mostly built in the 19th century. Typical of Hijazi architecture are the ornately carved overhanging balconies known as *rawshan*. The elaborate wooden fretwork or simple lattices which covered the windows were designed to capture the passing breeze and to allow the women to watch what was going on below without being seen. Some of these traditional features have been successfully incorporated in a modern context into the Hyatt Hotel.

Nassif House is one of the best preserved of the old houses and is now being restored as a museum and library. The tree by the front door used to be the only one in Jeddah, so that letters would always be addressed to the House of the Tree. Ibn Saud once stayed here, and it is said that, thanks to the wide ramps inside, despatch riders could go straight up on to the roof mounted on their camels to deliver their messages.

And, of course, there are always the **markets.** The Bedouin Souk specializes in headcloths, head ropes and the traditional robe called the *thawb*. You may also find some interesting silver amulets with Koranic inscriptions. Or visit the Yemeni Gold Souk, a familiar feature of every Saudi town. Bab Sharif Souk is more of a craft centre offering pots, baskets and cashmere shawls. Get up early in the morning to visit the fish market.

The Airport Souk comes alive at the time of the Hajj when pilgrims trade jewellery, carpets and other goods brought from home. This is the time when the cosmopolitan atmosphere of Jeddah really comes into its own, but the ordinary visitor may find it too crowded.

Before leaving, it is worth treating yourself to a bird's-eye view of the city from the water tower in the **Khuzam Palace gardens.**

Around Jeddah

The Red Sea coral reef which runs north and south of Jeddah has the richest marine life in the world, comparable to Australia's Great Barrier Reef. The reef is an underwater paradise for snorkelling and scuba-diving. Boat trips from Jeddah harbour can easily be arranged, but there are plenty of places which are accessible by car.

Sharm Abhur, known as "The Creek", is a popular seaside playground 50 kilometres north of Jeddah. Pierced by inlets which create calm lagoons, this stretch of water is ideal for water sports of all kinds and serves as a perfect respite from the heat of the city.

The Creek's edge is a shallow coral table which drops abruptly to a considerable depth several hundred metres out. The reef acts as a barrier to sharks, but there is a danger of poisoning from the well-camouflaged stonefish, so it is advisable to wear rubber-soled shoes. The water is wonderfully clear, accentuating the pink and purple coral and revealing myriad darting fish of all sizes, shapes and colours.

If you feel like a picnic in the shade, aim for **Wadi Khulays** on the road to USFAN, off the main route to Medina. This verdant region with its tall tamarisk trees is a bird-watcher's paradise. **Wadi Fatima** can be reached from the village of AL JUMUM by taking a track north for about 17 kilometres past palm gardens. Banana, guava and lemon trees grow along the banks of the irrigation channels and the air is full of the flight and song of birds.

Red Sea fishermen return at dawn with their bounty.

Ta'if

Some 150 kilometres inland from Jeddah, a wall of mountains rises sharply from the steaming plain and the air suddenly becomes fresh and cool. Nestling among these rocky hills is the town of Ta'if, 1,700 metres above sea level, a favoured spot for a weekend outing from Jeddah.

After the tedium of the "Christian By-pass" which skirts Mecca, the road snakes up a vertical escarpment affording magnificent views. The area abounds in bird and animal life, so you may catch a glimpse of a furtive fox, bright blue lizards or, if you're very lucky, the great manes of adult male baboons.

South of Ta'if, smooth boulders have been sculpted into strange shapes by the wind, and wild plants, trees and bushes grow freely among them. Euphorbias lift their succulent stems like weird candelabra, and groves of tamarisk, acacia, olive and juniper offer welcome patches of shade. The land is cultivated by families living in single-storey cottages built of stone. Everywhere there are fertile valleys growing almonds, apricots, figs, peaches and pomegranates, as well as all kinds of vegetables and cereals. In summer the fruit of the prickly pear is sold by the roadside.

Ta'if is more than just a holiday resort. It is also the summer capital where the king and his government spend two or three of the hottest months of the year. The wide streets are tree-lined and there are some fine modern, as well as old, buildings.

The main attraction is definitely the **souk,** probably the most authentic in the Hijaz. Behind the Aziziyah Hotel, in a warren of innumerable alleys lined with shops, you'll find tents, carpets, Bedouin handicrafts, traditional embroidered dresses and all the spices of an oriental market.

The towns surrounding Ta'if are also very inviting, but Al Shifa and Hadda particularly deserve a visit. **Al Shifa,** 3,000 metres above sea level, is a 20-kilometre drive from Ta'if. The best time to visit is in March when the spring rains have brought new life to the vegetation. **Hadda** at the tip of the escarpment road is equally picturesque. Both towns are built of stone with slim watchtowers standing out on the horizon. The dramatic views, the variety of flora and fauna and the cool crisp climate make these hill stations an attractive retreat from desert and coastal living.

North of Jeddah

This area is of special interest to archaeology buffs. A possible starting-point would be **Yanbu,** once a quiet port serving Medina and now Saudi Arabia's most important industrial centre alongside Jubayl. It has a new port, oil refinery, petrochemicals plant and subsidiary industries. The gas and crude oil pipelines which cross 1,000 kilometres of desert from the Eastern Province feed this vast development programme which already accommodates over half a million people.

This is all a far cry from T.E. Lawrence's description of Yanbu as "half a city of the dead"

Avant-garde design is a feature of many new Saudi buildings.

when he used it as a base in 1916 for his raids on the **Hijaz railway.** The railway line was only in operation for about ten years from its completion in 1908 and was built by the Turks to run from Damascus to Medina following the old pilgrim route. The aim was not to provide transport for the devout, but to supply food and ammunition to the troops. Attacks by the Bedouin who objected to this invasion of their territory **77** were stepped up by the addition of British recruits under Lawrence's banner. His raids under cover of darkness were facilitated by the mountainous terrain which offered immediate cover. Trains and stations were blown up and the Turkish garrison in Medina was cut off. Thus ended the short but dramatic life of the Hijaz railway.

A new road north of KHAYBAR to Al Ula runs parallel to a large section of the line for about 130 kilometres starting at ZUMMURUD. Phantom station-fortresses still stand mutely in the desert, sometimes with abandoned trains pulled up alongside. Elsewhere locomotives lie on the sand, the victims of a mine or an attack by Lawrence and his raiders. The stations, built out of large blocks of basalt, are on two floors with a central courtyard. They are mostly in good repair and make excellent camping areas. Of special note are SULTANIYAH with its own barracks, and HADIYA, AL BUWAYR and ABU AN NAAM, all of which have fully preserved locomotives.

Al Ula (mentioned in the Bible as Dedan), an oasis in the cleft of a magnificent red sandstone gorge, is an attractive mud-built town surrounded by orange orchards and palm groves. To the north, inscriptions in ancient script have been etched into the sandy cliffs, and there are tomb-like openings, some with carved lions.

These pre-date the more elaborate site of **Mada'in Salih**, once the southern capital of the Nabateans, whose base was Petra in Jordan. It was a key point on the caravan route sup-

plying incense and spices to Egypt, Palestine and the Mediterranean. The golden cliffs have been eroded into strange mushroom shapes and carved into ornate family tombs between 1 B.C. and A.D. 76. Inscriptions in a form of late Aramaic above the doors help to specify the date.

The *qala'a* or fort near the station is a good place to start your exploration of the site. To the east is a group of tombs which includes the **Qasr al Bint**

The cliffs near Al Ula bear evidence of its ancient history.

Dates, the staple of the Bedouin, are rich in nourishment.

("Maiden's Palace"). Though unfinished, it is a superb example of the stone-mason's craft, as is the **Bait ash Shaikh** ("House of the Sheikh") further to the south.

Permission to visit the site must first be obtained from the Department of Antiquities and Museums in Riyadh. When you reach Al Ula, forms must be presented to the Emir, and at Mada'in Salih, you must call in at the railway station where the local policeman keeps a list of prospective visitors. The museum near the town hall in Al Ula provides useful background information.

From monuments to the dead to a record of daily life around 4,000 B.C.: 20 kilometres east of HANAKIYAH some fascinating **prehistoric carvings** are to be found. Look out for a red outcrop of rock to the north of the main road. One large rock with sheer sides has a number of friezes showing ibex, gazelle, dogs and human figures, but the oldest and most remarkable of these carvings portrays long-horned cattle which have not been seen in Arabia for thousands of years.

The Holy Cities

Mecca "the Blessed" and Medina "the Radiant" have been holy sites since the time of Muhammad (and Mecca even earlier), so the Saudis see themselves as guardians of tradition, as well as protectors of the faith. Both cities are strictly banned to non-Muslims, but most visitors, even if they are not allowed inside, will want to know something of what lies within.

Mecca

Mecca is the religious capital of Saudi Arabia and of all the Islamic world. Known as Umm al Qurrah, "Mother of Cities", it is the place from which Islam sprang and towards which every believer faces five times a day in prayer. And for millions of Muslims it is the goal of a lifetime, the centre of the world's biggest pilgrimage, the Hajj.

For some the Hajj may mean a journey across half the globe, representing years of saving and sacrifice. Participation in the ceremonies in and around Mecca constitutes an affirmation of fundamental beliefs and re-dedication to these principles, a kind of rebirth. It is also a symbol of brotherhood and unity.

The **Sacred Mosque,** at the centre of Mecca, can accommodate 300,000 people and encloses the **Ka'aba,** the cubic "House of God" built by the Prophet Abraham. The Ka'aba, covered with a black pall woven with excerpts from the Koran in gold thread, incorporates a holy black stone revered since the time of Abraham; some believe that the stone dates back to Adam. Nearby lie the tombs of Hagar and her son Ishmael, as well as the footprint of Abraham and the Well of Zamzam. The present-day mosque also includes a vast corridor linking two hills, Safa and Marwah.

Though steeped in tradition, Mecca is now a modern city with facilities to cater for 2 million pilgrims a year. Special areas are provided and there is a good bus service. At the time of the Hajj, many pilgrims also stay in Jeddah.

Medina

In Islam, Medina ranks next to Mecca in importance, because its inhabitants invited the Prophet to come and live among them when the Meccans had turned their backs on him (see p. 32). The city lies 445 kilometres from Mecca and about 425 kilometres from Jeddah.

The journey there, about five or six hours by road, takes the pilgrim through the history of early Islam. Approaching from the Red Sea, the first stop is **Badr,** a village where the Muslims won their first battle against the Meccans. Winding through wind-swept hills, the road passes **Quba** where stands

the simple whitewashed building of the Prophet's Mosque. In Medina itself are many other mosques, including the **Qiblatayn,** where Muhammad first changed the direction of prayer from Jerusalem to Mecca.

The **Mosque of the Prophet** *(Masjid ash Sharif),* topped by a green dome, is in the centre of the city. Muhammad's tomb, below the dome, is surrounded by a grill, which also encloses the tombs of the first two orthodox caliphs, Abu Bakr and Umar. The tomb attributed to the Prophet's daughter, Fatima, is in fact empty; she is buried in the graveyard across the street. The Prophet was buried in his own house, around which a mosque grew to enclose the dwelling.

An itinerary for visiting the mosque, called the *ziyyara,* with its own recitations, has developed over the centuries. It begins at the Bab as Salam (Gate of Peace) and stops off at many other points besides the tombs themselves.

Pilgrims of all ages flock to Mecca for the Hajj. After donning the garments of ihram *(restriction), they circle the Ka'aba seven times.*

The South-West

Asir

The mountain garden of Saudi Arabia, the Asir region is the site of the country's first national park. It has always been fairly inaccessible, as its name "Difficult Country" suggests. This accounts for the distinctive character of the people, their architecture, customs and dress.

Assimilated by Ibn Saud into his kingdom in 1927, the Asir, encompassing more than 2,000 villages, was frequently the scene of intertribal hostilities. Firearms are still part of the Asiri mode of dress and the people retain a fierce pride and independence of spirit. They cling to their traditions, but even here the benefits of oil-based development can now be seen in the form of widespread irrigation schemes, schools, hospitals, new housing and roads.

There are frequent flights from Jeddah and Riyadh to **Abha,** the main town of the province and a good base from which to explore this unusual region. The Visitor Centre here provides the best introduction to the terrain and wildlife, as well as details of hiking paths and campsites.

Abha is a gracious town perched at a height of 2,200 metres in the heart of a chain of mountains, the Sarawat, that climb towards the Yemen. The climate is delightfully cool and the frequent rains nourish an abundant plant life. Small villages with terraced farms cluster on the hill tops. Watchtowers that dot the horizon tell of a troubled and inse-

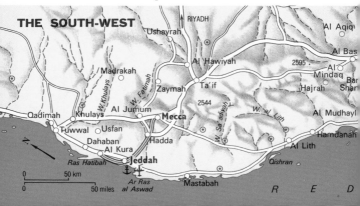

THE SOUTH-WEST

cure past when farmers had to be ready at any moment to run to these fortifications to seek refuge from raiders. The squat houses are painted in bright colours, and a practical and time-honoured architectural feature can be seen in the slabs of slate built into the walls to deflect the rain and provide shade in summer.

Although there is modern housing, some well-maintained examples of the old style still remain. A covered souk sells everything but food, while the colourful main market on Tuesdays has hundreds of stalls selling fruit and vegetables; melons and pomegranates are a speciality. The Bedouin often come here to sell their goats and sheep. The most distinctive of the local tribes are the Tuhama, valley dwellers, of short wiry build with gaunt, striking faces and long curly hair oiled with butter. They wear an *izar* (skirt) and carry tasselled short swords. The unveiled Tuhama women are noted for their high-crowned straw hats, while those from other tribes wear flat-crowned, wide-brimmed headgear. An older woman might wear a *mi'zar* (cape) of goatskin.

In the market-place remain vestiges of a folklore that has disappeared from other parts of the country. Interesting items for sale include deep metal buckets which hold a clay *tanoor* (portable bread oven), and sprigs of *raihan,* a sweet-smelling green plant which is put in water to refresh a room or made into head circlets by the country children.

The city is destined to form

the cornerstone of a tourist industry and will feature modern hotels and a golf course. The 450,000 hectares of national park is intended to protect endangered species, as well as to provide camping sites, picnic areas and hiking trails. More than 300 bird species can be spotted in this haven for bird-watchers.

A drive to **Jabal Sawdah,** the escarpment which falls steeply to the Red Sea, is a worthwhile circular trip from Abha, taking about two hours. Turn off the Ta'if road after 17 kilometres and you will pass along WADI AL ATIF, sheltering a number of typical stone-built villages. Some are only connected by dirt tracks but a two-wheel-drive vehicle is sufficient if you don't mind a rough and dusty ride. Defensive watchtowers, often sited on a commanding peak, are a striking feature of the landscape. From Jabal Sawdah there is a magnificent view of terraced fields supported by stone walls and extensive juniper forest. The highest point is at 3,300 metres.

A descent to the **Tihamah** coastal plain is an adventure

The Saudis have cultivated every available inch of fertile land.

into another Arabia. The mountain range has always acted as a cultural barrier. Here in the sultry plain a slow-moving, rural way of life has remained unchanged for centuries.

The beach at **Ash Shuqayq** is very popular, as are the lagoons strung along the coast where you are likely to see herons, pelicans and flamingoes. In addition to bird-watching, the coastline is ideal for fishing and coral diving.

For those with less time, some villages like **An Nisab** in the vicinity of Abha are astonishingly well preserved and worth investigating. **Mohalah,** between Abha and Khamis, boasts fish-filled pools, and **Qarrah,** 30 kilometres further south, has a palace built by Ibn Saud. Since the area forms part of the Asir National Park, you'll find camping facilities and hiking trails. Baboons can be seen scampering about in large groups in the valleys.

Some 50 kilometres south of Abha lies **Habalah,** "Rope Valley" as it is locally known. The deep escarpment once sheltered a farming settlement, and access could only be gained by a precipitous path or with rope ladders *(habal).*

While Abha is the capital of a vast recreation area, **Khamis,** 87 known as the "Jewel of Asir", is a thriving city at the heart of rich farmland. The high annual rainfall and temperate climate make this one of the most fertile areas in the Kingdom.

The town is also a charming mixture of old and new. Traditional stone or mud houses with heavy painted doors made of wood or cast iron sit side by side with modern developments. Expansion has been rapid due to the King Faisal Military City and the King Khalid Air Base. These new installations account for an increasingly cosmopolitan population. Communications with the rest of the country are excellent both by air and by an improving network of roads connecting Abha with Riyadh, Jeddah and Jaizan in the south.

Khamis used to be known as Khamis Mushayt after the governors of the town since the 1920s. It is known for its colourful **market** which takes place every *khamis* (Thursday) in the centre of town. The merchants have a reputation for being astute businessmen, a claim borne out by the wealth of shops and supermarkets, not to mention the stalls set out on market day. Behind the neat rows of fruit and vegetables, the aroma of spices fills the air. Women sit cross-legged beside

baskets brimming with cloves, cardamom, henna, frankincense and myrrh. These Bedouin women also sell good silver jewellery at more reasonable prices than in the big cities.

The stalls nearby sell baskets unique to the area. They are shaped like urns with turquoise and burgundy designs on them and usually have conical lids reminiscent of the *Arabian Nights*. There are mats, too, and wide-brimmed straw hats as worn by the sheep-herding women of the Asir—in fact, everything from ancient sewing-machines to the ornamental daggers still worn by the men. The more exotic valley dwellers can be identified by their coloured head-bands.

There is a pre-Islamic settlement (possibly Nabatean) at **Jarash,** 16 kilometres out of Khamis. As it is an archaeological site, permission must be obtained before visiting it. Two kilometres away on an extinct volcano called the Black Mountain, there are some ancient inscriptions and rock drawings. The mud farmsteads of the villages along the

The South-West has its own particular customs, styles of dress and architecture.

Wadi Tindahah are a prelude to yet another style of building in the adjoining province of Najran.

Najran

The houses of Najran are an echo of ancient Akkad and Sumer. Resembling those of Abha, they have a steadfastness and purity of style that has survived four millennia. The mud is rammed on in layers and then dried, creating the characteristic ridges. They can be from five to eight storeys high —the further south you go the taller they become. Many of the town houses even have stained-glass windows.

The old **Emir's palace** in the town of **Najran** is one of the most handsome examples of this style of architecture—a fairy-tale castle with square towers and decorative crenellations on the turrets. It is a style much seen in the Yemen and reappears in the *kasbahs* of Morocco. The custom of painting white decorative outlines around doors and windows can also be observed in southern Mauritania.

To the right of the vegetable souk in the centre of town is the **Bedouin market** where the Najran women sit under umbrellas selling spices, henna, silver jewellery and small bas-

kets. Like their houses, the people have a fairy-tale look —the men with the *jambiyya* (silver dagger) in their belts and the women brightly dressed, some with blue tattoo marks on their chins.

Before the 6th century, Najran was a Christian centre. It became the scene of dramatic

90

A fairy-tale castle? The Emir of Najran holds court in this palace built of clay.

events when one of its rulers, Dhu Nuwas, attempted to convert the Christians to his own religion, Judaism. In the year 522, the choice was put before the inhabitants: convert or die. They chose the latter and were thrown into a burning trench. The Koran holds up the martyrs of Najran as an example of strength of faith. The remains of their city, now called Ukhdud (The Trench), lie on the south side of the wadi. Permission is needed to visit the site.

What to Do

Sports

Even the most familiar activities will take on a new dimension in the eternal sunshine of the Arabian Peninsula. So, try to escape from the city as often as possible to sample the splendours of the great outdoors; camping in the desert, riding a pure-bred Arab horse and sailing in the Red Sea or the Gulf will be unforgettable experiences.

In the coastal areas the possibilities for water sports are endless and facilities continue to expand. The beaches are superb and the water is deliciously warm. You can enjoy sailing, wind-surfing, swimming, fishing, water-skiing, snorkeling and scuba-diving all year round. Renting a dhow is a fun and exotic way of visiting the islands in the Gulf.

Deep-sea fishing enthusiasts can catch *qidd* (barracuda) and *kan'ad* (mackerel) in the Gulf, and tuna, red snapper and sea bass in the Red Sea. Rods and reels are available locally.

You'll find facilities for golf and tennis through companies and private clubs. The large hotels often have tennis courts available at single admission or season rates. Many villas have private pools, but most public swimming pools are open to men only. Several riding stables in Riyadh and Jeddah organize instruction, gymkhanas and show jumping.

In Jeddah you can join the Jeddah Squash League, the Dunes Club (tennis, squash, cricket, golf and handball; for Jeddah residents only), Al Hamra Fitness Club or the Jeddah Euro Motorcross Association. Sports clubs in Riyadh include the Hash House Harriers (non-competitive running), Road Runners, Desert Golf Club, Riyadh Squash League, Riyadh Bowling Centre and the Oasis Sub-Aqua Club.

There is horse racing at Riyadh stadium during the winter season. More topical, though, is camel racing; and the high point of the year is undoubtedly the King's Camel Race held in April or May north-east of Riyadh. Thousands of *dhaluls,* riding camels, are entered for the race, in which they run a long course in the desert—for substantial prizes.

The King's Camel Race is a closely contested event.

The Art of Falconry

Three thousand years ago, hunters in the Middle East were already pursuing quarry with birds of prey: an ancient Assyrian carving shows a falconer carrying a hawk on his wrist. Today falconry is one of the most popular and skilled sports in Saudi Arabia.

Peregrines and saker falcons are the favourite. Dramatic performers, they fly high above their prey before diving on it from above. They either strike the bird to the ground with a blow from a powerful talon or seize it in mid-air.

In training, young falcons are attached to a perch and taught to fly onto a gloved hand to feed and be gently stroked and cajoled. Then they learn to fly at a piece of weighted meat twirled on a line at ever-increasing distances. Finally they fly free to attack game, always returning to the wrist. When not hunting, falcons are kept hooded to keep them quiet. Little bells tied to their legs signal their whereabouts.

The numbers of houbara bustard and other game were rapidly diminishing at one time in Saudi Arabia through the use of firearms. But hunting with guns is now banned and only falconry or coursing is allowed.

Entertainment

Even in the absence of public theatres and cinemas, there is plenty to do to fill your leisure time. Social life is active and there are numerous amateur theatrical, music and sports groups. The Riyadh International Women's Group is helpful for orientation and provides a variety of activities for members.

Video is now the ideal form of home entertainment and there are shops selling equipment and films in the major cities. Some television sets can receive two or three of the existing broadcast systems including the one used in Saudi Arabia, but check with your dealer before hiring or purchasing.

With time to spare, a trip into the desert either for a picnic or a long weekend will reward you with spectacular sunrises and sunsets, the hospitality of a Bedouin encampment or even the discovery of an archaeological site. One word of warning—it is forbidden to pocket your finds. The Saudis are proud of their past and are in the process of preserving its traces. But you can of course start your own dig, for desert roses or other fossils. To learn more about the desert, join The Desert Ramblers in Riyadh. Details of meetings are usually given in the *Arab News*.

Museums are always an interesting way of learning about a country and its past. Of special note are the Museum of Archaeology and Ethnography and the Folkore Museum (see p. 43), both in Riyadh. Living folklore such as the Ardah sword dance can be seen on television or at the occasional festival organized by one of the big hotels (which also sponsor art, jewellery and photographic exhibitions).

The universities offer shows, exhibits and other entertainment. The English-language newspapers carry announcements of all such activities.

Falconry has its adherents among the topmost Saudis.

Shopping

In Saudi Arabia, shopping is a form of entertainment and should be embarked upon in this spirit, especially in the souks where there is so much to delight the senses and tempt the purse. Prices are not fixed, so you will be expected to negotiate, a skill much prized by the Arabs.

Electronic goods, cameras and watches can often be good value, especially in the markets, but the main attractions for most visitors are naturally the antique or traditional items. *Siniyat* or brass trays in all sizes make an attractive addition to any room. Another favourite is the *dillah* or coffee pot; the antique ones have a more mellow patina.

To complete the set you might feel like acquiring the small coffee cups, a pestle and mortar or even a *mihmas,* the skillet with a long-handled stirrer for roasting the beans. A *narguilah* or hubble-bubble pipe is certainly a conversation piece even if you don't intend to use it.

One of the richest sights of today's cities are the gold souks where the stalls display a glittering array of rings, bracelets and chains. Prices are fixed by weight rather than workmanship. Pearls from the Gulf

are exquisite—and reasonably priced, too. Gold has begun to replace silver as the chosen jewellery of the Bedouin. Good pieces of silver are therefore becoming more difficult to find and many old well-worn pieces are renovated by "dipping". Some of the finest silverwork can be found on the sheaths of

Bedouin women at their spinning; the wool is woven into colourful draperies and carpets.

daggers, the most popular of which is the curved *khanjar.* The *jambiyya* and *saif,* short and long swords, are likewise decorated with semi-precious stones.

Ornately carved chests, doors and lattice-work are a feature of western Arabia, but the Saudis' desire to preserve these antiques means that they may not be exported.

Weaving remains a traditional craft for the women of Saudi Arabia. They weave striped tents, as well as rugs, bags and **97**

camel trappings. Leather bags decorated with fringes and tassels are particularly colourful in the Ta'if region.

If you feel tempted to buy a carpet, be careful. A lot of carpets are not made in Saudi Arabia. Prayer mats, however, usually are, and those that have been hand-woven by the Bedouin using natural dyes are the most valuable. Here are some guidelines for authenticating a good carpet. The colours should glow but not be garish and the pile should be deep. This can be checked by counting the knots on the reverse side with the help of a ruler. The best quality carpets will have three to four hundred knots per square inch (6½ sq. cm).

Certain items of clothing make comfortable and practical home wear—the long shirt known as a *thawb*, for instance, and the head cloths which can be worn as scarves.

All the perfumes of Arabia will waft your way from the stalls of the *attarin*—among them rose water, jasmine and musk. But the most precious is *oud*, wood of aloes burnt over charcoal in very small quantities.

The ornate curved jambiyya dagger is part of traditional Arab dress.

Eating Out

The way food is cooked and eaten reflects many facets of the Arab character and way of life. They are social activities deeply rooted in the Bedouin tradition whereby any traveller could demand food and shelter for up to three days.

When you are invited to a Saudi home, you will be able to observe this warmth and generosity and appreciate the more traditional dishes which may be served, whereas other Middle Eastern food, as well as familiar international dishes, tend to be the standard fare in hotels and restaurants.

A picnic or a beach party is the nearest you will get to a traditional Arab feast. The food is laid out on mats or carpets and there may not be knives or forks. The main dish may be a young camel or sheep boiled or roasted, served with rice and a variety of side dishes. The host usually walks around making sure his guests are well looked after. Water, soap and towels are provided for hand-washing after the meal; rose water or cologne may also be available. Often the first group of guests make room for a second and the children and servants eat last.

Bargaining

In an economy where many products are handmade, each item has a different value depending on the quality of workmanship. Bargaining is thus a way of determining the proper price, not simply a way for a shopkeeper to get more money from one customer than from the next. To reach the best price though, you must get to know the market by browsing in several shops and asking the price of comparable pieces.

However, bargaining in the souks is more than a means of determining price. It's a time-honoured social ritual as well, in which skills at negotiation are put to the test. You should emphasize the bad points of your prospective purchase and the shopkeeper will retaliate with the good ones. A compromise should be reached—in your favour.

Should you find that your skills are no match for those of the souk shopkeepers, remember that other than the souks most shops and supermarkets have fixed prices so there is no question of bargaining, and you may well find what you want there.

Appetizers

Just to whet your appetite, you'll be tempted by all kinds of *mezze,* one of the most delightful features of Middle Eastern food. Indeed these succulent morsels can almost turn into a meal in themselves. There are nuts of all kinds, roasted melon seeds, and dips for the flat round unleavened bread. *Hummus* made from chick peas or *tahinah* from sesame meal paste, as well as an aubergine puree, are particularly popular. Then there are a host of miniature foods like meat balls *(kuftah),* savoury pastries and vine leaves *(waraq aynab)* stuffed with rice and meat.

Main Courses

The favourite meal of the Bedouin has long been *saliq,* lamb cooked in spiced milk and served on a bed of rice, though this is basic desert fare. *Mihammar* is slightly more sophisticated and consists of stuffed lamb cooked in a yoghurt sauce. Many different kinds of stuffing are used, mostly consisting of nuts, raisins and other dried fruit.

Kabbza, usually lamb but sometimes chicken, is cooked with onion, tomato and cucumber to which grated carrot, orange rind and other fruit may be added. Cloves, cinnamon and cardamom are favourite spices, though the food is generally not highly seasoned. Ghee, a kind of clarified butter of an oily consistency, is often used.

One of the great dishes served for New Year in Mecca, and a genuine delicacy if you can find it, is *thurid,* chicken in a cream sauce served on very fine leaves of dough. *Shurba,* a substantial soup, often accompanied by *sambusik,* triangular wafers with a spicy meat and onion filling fried in oil, is the choice for breaking Ramadan. *Burghul* or cracked wheat in a stew staves off the pangs of hunger during the fast.

If you find yourself near the coast you won't be able to resist the shrimp, and the black seabream garnished with a touch of ginger is also a delicacy.

Rice is the usual accompaniment to meat and fish dishes and flavoured with saffron, cumin or pine nuts.

Aubergines, onions, peppers and carrots can be found in the markets. Courgettes, cabbages and onions are often stuffed and *okra* (ladies' fingers) are served in a tomato sauce. A favourite side salad is cucumber with yoghurt and mint. Lettuce and tomato salads may come flavoured with orange blossom water.

Desserts

Sweetmeats are always kept ready for the unexpected guest. At a time of festivity, they are in abundance. There are as many variations of *baklava* as there are of pancakes, and rice pudding is served cold with cinnamon and blanched almonds.

As a refreshing change for breakfast why not try *labna*, cream cheese made into a tart or simply shaped into little balls and rolled in paprika. Other pastries may not have orig- inated in Saudi Arabia, but they are certainly delicious and death to any diet.

The choice of fresh fruit is almost endless: melons, water-melons, pomegranates, grapes, bananas, peaches, apricots. Some fruits are stewed or stuffed. But the ceremonial offering of welcome has always

An Arab feast: kabbza *lamb, vegetables, bread and fruit make a lavish spread.*

The coffee ceremony begins with the preparation of the beans.

been the date. Whether they are red or black, they have a mouth-watering flavour and high nutritional value—as the Bedouin have known for centuries.

Drinks

If you are a coffee drinker, then you have come to its homeland and need stray no further than the nearest coffee house to sample its unique aroma and taste. The ritual of preparation and drinking is as important as the brew itself.

In a Bedouin tent or an

skillet over a fire. The coffee is then ground with a pestle and brewed in a pot while the cardamom is prepared in another pot. Finally, the two are mixed together to produce a green-coloured, somewhat bitter drink quite different from Turkish coffee. Cloves or saffron can also be added. The coffee is served from brass pots with long spouts stuffed with fibre to strain the grains and is drunk from small tumblers without handles. Three servings are normal. To accept less would be considered impolite; noisy sipping indicates appreciation. Give your cup a slight twist or shake when you have had enough.

Sweet Turkish coffee is more prevalent in cities, and mint, as well as ordinary sweet tea, are also available. Men gather for refreshment and conversation in the ubiquitous coffee houses, where the hubble-bubble or water pipe *(narguilah)* is passed around.

Other beverages consist of all kinds of bottled soft drinks and fresh fruit juices. *Laban* is a deliciously refreshing mixture of yoghurt and water flavoured with salt and crushed mint. All alcohol is banned, but alcohol-free beer is popular. Camel milk is appreciated by connoisseurs.

emir's palace, offering coffee is the most usual form of hospitality and represents the host's obligation to protect his guest. It is served at any time of day but particularly in the mornings, when business can be settled over a cup of coffee.

In the desert, the beans are lightly toasted in a long-handled

To Help You Order...

I would like a/an/some...   *abghaa*   أبغى

bill, check	*al hisaab*	الحساب	lemon	*laymoon*	ليمون
bread	*zubdah*	زبدة	meat	*lahm*	لحم
butter	*khubz*	خبز	milk	*haleeb*	حليب
cheese	*jubnah*	جبنة	mineral water	*maay ma'danee*	مياه معدنية
coffee	*qahwah*	قهوة	mustard	*mistardah*	مستردة
dessert	*halwah*	حلوة	salad	*salaatah*	صلطة
egg	*bayd*	بيض	salt	*milh*	ملح
fish	*samak*	سمك	soup	*shurbah*	شوربة
fruit	*fawaakih*	فواكه	sugar	*sukkar*	سكر
fruit juice	*aseer*	عصير	tea	*shay*	شاي
			yoghurt	*laban*	لبن

...and Read the Menu

عدس	*adas*	lentils	كفتة	*kuftah*	meat balls
أرز	*aruzz*	rice	مقلي	*maqlee*	fried
باذنجان	*baadinjaan*	aubergine	مشوي	*mashwee*	grilled
بصل	*basal*	onions	مسلوق	*maslooq*	boiled
بطاطس	*bataatis*	potatoes	موز	*mawz*	banana
بطيخ	*bateekh*	watermelon	مهلبية	*muhallabeeya*	rice pudding
دجاج	*dajaaj*	chicken	شمام	*shamaam*	musk melon
فلفل	*filfil*	peppers			
فستق	*fustuq*	pistachio nuts	طماطم	*tamaatim*	tomato
حمص	*hummus*	chick peas	تمر	*tamr*	date
خروف	*kharoof*	lamb	ثوم	*thoom*	garlic
خوخ	*khookh*	peaches			

How to Get There

The information given below is liable to change at any moment. It is best, therefore, to consult an informed travel agent well before your departure.

BY AIR

From the British Isles: Regular flights leave Heathrow for Jeddah, Riyadh and Dhahran. Types of fare: first-class, economy, club, youth (12–24), student (24–28), excursion. High and low season and special fares are also available. Flight time: approximately 6½ hours.

From North America: Scheduled flights link Dhahran, Jeddah and Riyadh with various U.S. cities, either direct or via New York. Types of fare: first-class, economy and excursion fares are available from Canada. From the U.S.A. you can travel first-class, economy, excursion, APEX, Affinity Group or seasonal excursion. Flight time New York–Jeddah: approximately 12 hours.

From Australia: There are no direct flights to Saudi Arabia from any city in Australia, but connections are possible via various gateways in the Far East and Middle East. Types of fare: first-class, economy and excursion.

From New Zealand: No direct flights link New Zealand with Saudi Arabian cities, but connections are possible via various gateways in the Far East and Middle East. Types of fare: first-class, economy and excursion.

BY SEA

There are regular sailings, including a car ferry, from Suez to Jeddah and Yanbu. Shipping services also operate between Hodeidah (Yemen Arab Republic) and Jeddah. Other ports with shipping links to Jeddah are Port Sudan (Sudan) and Berbera (Somali Republic).

Cargo boats with some cabins leave for Jeddah from Marseille and other French ports, as well as Barcelona and Genoa. There is no regular service, but further information can be obtained from shipping guides.

When to Go

Times to avoid are the Hajj season and Ramadan, the dates of which vary from year to year (see Calendar p. 110).

From May to October, temperatures can reach well over 40°C (120°F) in most parts of the Peninsula. On the coast, temperatures may be lower, but the humidity adds to discomfort. A northerly wind called the *shamaal,* which can blow up into violent sandstorms, is most prevalent in late spring, early summer. There is air-conditioning in most hotels, shops and restaurants. The cooler months from November to April are much more pleasant with balmy days. Nights can get a little chilly—even freezing in the desert and some mountain regions.

Average daily maximum temperatures

		J	F	M	A	M	J	J	A	S	O	N	D
Riyadh	°F	70	73	82	89	100	107	107	107	102	94	84	70
	°C	21	23	28	32	38	42	42	42	39	34	29	21
Jeddah	°F	84	84	85	91	95	97	99	99	96	95	91	86
	°C	29	29	29	33	35	36	37	37	36	35	33	30

Planning Your Budget

To give you an idea of what to expect, here are some average prices in Saudi Riyals. However, take into account that all prices must be regarded as approximate. Note also that most prices concern services of an international standard as provided by large hotels. In some cases there are also parallel services on the popular level, including hotels and restaurants with correspondingly lower prices.

Airport Transfer. *Riyadh* airport to city centre, taxi SR 50. *Jeddah* airport to city centre, taxi SR 60. *Dhahran,* taxi from airport to Al Khobar SR 30; to Damman SR 40. Porter SR 2 per bag.

Car Hire. *Honda Civic* SR 85 per day, including 100 free kilometres, SR 00.25 per kilometre above that, SR 510 per week with unlimited mileage. *Datsun 180B* SR 120 per day, including 100 free kilometres, SR 00.35 per kilometre above that, SR 720 per week with unlimited mileage. *Chevrolet Caprice* SR 170 per day, including 100 free kilometres, SR 00.50 per kilometre above that, SR 1,020 per week with unlimited mileage. Chauffeur (8-hour day): SR 80 over normal car-hire rates; overtime SR 15 per hour.

Cigarettes. SR 25 per packet.

Fuel. SR 00.22 per litre of petrol.

Hairdressers. Haircut SR 30. Shampoo and set SR 20–40. Tip 10%.

Hotels (double room with bath per night). Luxury class SR 400, first class SR 360, second class SR 240, simple SR 150. All hotels add 15% service charge and an additional charge for telephone calls and telex.

Meals and Drinks. Continental breakfast SR 15–25; lunch/dinner in international hotel SR 75–100; coffee and tea SR 5 in hotels; water and soft drinks SR 4–8 in hotels, SR 1 in grocery stores and cafés.

Newspapers. National SR 1; international SR 2–5.

Shopping Bag. Bread (½ kg.) SR 2–4; butter (½ kg.) SR 11; cheese (imported; ½ kg.) SR 32; potatoes (1 kg.) SR 3; beefsteak (1 kg.) SR 42; coffee (¼ kg.) SR 11; milk (1 litre) SR 4; beer without alcohol SR 3.

Transport. *Taxis:* at least SR 10 and up for yellow cabs. Large air-conditioned cabs which wait outside hotels are a minimum of SR 30. *Buses:* within the city SR 1; intercity SR 10–40.

BLUEPRINT for a Perfect Trip

An A-Z Summary of Practical Information and Facts

A star (*) following an entry indicates that relevant prices are to be found on page 107.

Listed after many entries is the appropriate Arabic translation, usually in the singular, plus a number of phrases that should help you when seeking assistance.

Contents

AIRPORTS *(matáar)**. Saudi Arabia has over 20 airports, of which Jeddah, Riyadh, Medina and Dhahran are international. SAUDIA, the national airline, operates frequent flights to the major cities within the country (see under TRANSPORT), as well as flying international routes.

Riyadh. King Khalid International Airport, 35 km. north of the city centre, is a stunning piece of modern architecture in a magnificent setting of landscaped greenery. Terminals for domestic and international flights are connected by automatic moving walkways. The link area contains shops, a post office, a bank and snack bars. There is also a medical infirmary and a mosque. Buses offer a half-hourly service between the airport and city centre.

Jeddah. King Abdul Aziz International Airport, 33 km. north of the city centre, has three terminals, one of which is entirely devoted to passengers performing the Hajj. All the normal facilities are offered, as well as prayer and rest areas and a guidance centre operated by the Ministry of Pilgrimage and Endowments. A free shuttle service operates between the terminals.

Dhahran International Airport lies 15 km. south-east of Dhahran and 10 km. from Al Khobar. A bus leaves every hour for Dammam and Al Khobar, and there is also a service to the domestic terminal some distance away.

There is no airport tax and no duty-free shop at any of the airports.

ARCHAEOLOGICAL SITES. Saudi Arabia has a number of places of archaeological interest, including Qaryat al Fau, Qarayyat al Milh, Al Ula, and Mada'in Salih. Several have local museums attached.

Visits to the sites are discouraged as they are poorly protected, but permission may be obtained from:

Director General, Department of Antiquities and Museums, P.O. Box 3734, Riyadh; tel. 435 5821.

The Department is housed in the same building as the Museum of Archaeology and Ethnography in Riyadh.

A form has to be completed and it may be some time before you hear whether permission has been granted or not, so it is best to plan well in advance. It is also recommended that you obtain the approval of the local authorities when you arrive at the site.

CALENDAR. The Islamic era (A.H. = Anno Hegirae) is dated from July 16, 622, the first day of the year in which the Hijrah took place. The calendar is made up of twelve lunar months corresponding to 354 days. Months start with the sighting of the new moon. The day begins at sunset and runs until sunset of the following day.

Islamic Calendar

A.H.	New Year (1st Muharram)	Mawlud (Prophet's Birthday)	Ramadan begins	Id al-Kibir (Day of Pilgrimage)
1405	27 Sep 1984	7 Dec 1984	21 May 1985	28 Aug 1985
1406	16 Sep 1985	26 Nov 1985	11 May 1986	17 Aug 1986
1407	6 Sep 1986	15 Nov 1986	30 Apr 1987	6 Aug 1987
1408	26 Aug 1987	5 Nov 1987	19 Apr 1988	26 July 1988
1409	14 Aug 1988	24 Oct 1988	8 Apr 1989	15 July 1989
1410	4 Aug 1989	14 Oct 1989	29 Mar 1990	5 July 1990
1411	24 July 1990	3 Oct 1990	18 Mar 1991	24 June 1991
1412	13 July 1991	22 Sep 1991	6 Mar 1992	12 June 1992

CAMPING *(mukháyyam)*. A few sites have been established along the Red Sea coast, but facilities are meagre. The Bedouin have been camping for centuries so, like them, you can make the desert your own.

CAR HIRE *(isti'jáar sayyáara)**. (See also DRIVING.) Large international firms as well as smaller agencies have cars for hire. Prices vary according to size and comfort. Popular smaller models may be difficult to obtain, so make a reservation from your country of departure.

Residents must have a valid Saudi licence. Visitors may drive with an international permit. Most car-hire firms stipulate a minimum age of 21 and will not accept a licence of less than one year's standing.

Chauffeur-driven cars are available and recommended for those unfamiliar with Saudi traffic.

I'd like to hire a car with driver.	**ábghaa astá'jir sayyáara ma'a sawwáag**

CIGARETTES, CIGARS, TOBACCO *(sagáayır, sigáar, dukháan)**. Most brands are on sale in stores. Smoking tends to be frowned upon, especially in the souks and in traditional households. Refrain from smoking in public during Ramadan.

A packet of …, please.	**'ílbit … min fádlak**
matches	**kibréet**

CLOTHING. Washable cottons or natural fibres are the most appropriate for the climate. Bring a good supply because the combination of hard water and strong sunlight does not prolong the life of clothes. Sunglasses and sunhats are essential, but don't forget that in Riyadh, for instance, it can get quite cold in winter and you will need warm clothes, which you should bring with you. Good shoes are expensive; stock up before you leave home and pack some good desert boots or plimsolls (sneakers). Women should dress conservatively outside the home: long dresses with sleeves, no plunging necklines, and no trousers. Saudi women cover their heads, but foreign women are not required to do so, although a head covering of some sort may come in useful. Shorts should not be worn except on the beach.

COMMUNICATIONS. Enormous expansion of the country's post, telex and telephone systems has taken place over recent years.

Post *(baréed).* There is no home delivery service. Mail is only delivered to government ministries and postal box numbers. Your mail should be sent to the post office box of your employer or contact in Saudi Arabia. You can apply for a personal postal box, but the waiting period may be lengthy. All mail is subject to censorship. Don't mail, or have mailed, items prohibited in the Kingdom.

Telephone *(tilifóon).* Local, long distance and most international calls can be dialled direct. There are telephone booths in major cities. Telex and telephone facilities are available in hotels at an extra charge.

Telex is a much-favoured means of long-distance communication.

I'd like some stamps, please.	**uréed tawáabi' minfádlak**
express (special delivery)	**bil baréed al-mustá'jil**
airmail	**bil baréed al-jawwée**
registered	**bil baréed al-musájjal**
Is there any mail for ...?	**fee baréed li ...**
May I use the telephone?	**múmkin astá'mil at-tilifóon**
Please can you help me get this number in ...?	**min fádlak, saa'ídnee fil ittisáal bi háadha ar-raqam fee ...**

COMPLAINTS. In shops, hotels or restaurants, ask to speak to the manager. A calm, courteous approach will be more likely to lead to an amicable solution, but deadlock can usually be broken by suggesting appeal to a higher authority. If you have a serious complaint, refer the matter to your embassy.

C **CONVERSION CHARTS.** (For fluid and distance measures see DRIVING.) Saudi Arabia uses the metric system.

Temperature

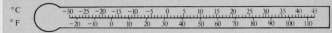

Length

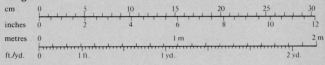

Weight

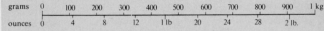

A traditional measure you may come across is the *ooghiya* or "ounce", which has various values in different Arab countries. In Saudi Arabia it is equivalent to 28.1 grams. The *ooghiya* is used for measuring small articles such as incense.

COURTESIES. Respecting Arab ways and conforming as far as possible to the customs of the country will go a long way towards smoothing your path (see p. 32). A smile and a few words of Arabic will work wonders.

CRIME and THEFT. Crime is relatively rare in Saudi Arabia and penalties are harsh. The law applies equally to Muslim and non-Muslim; as a foreigner you are not immune. Drink and drug offences are regarded very seriously. Offenders are held while the crime is being investigated. There is no *habeas corpus* and there are often long delays before a case is heard. Three month prison sentences are the minimum. Certain offences may result in instant deportation. As in other countries, offering a bribe is a criminal offence and is severely punished.

D **DRIVING IN SAUDI ARABIA.** A car is a necessity, but care and patience are the rules of the road. Traffic is congested in cities, so leave plenty of time for getting to appointments and to the airport.

An international driving permit is acceptable, as well as a valid

D

licence from most countries for up to 45 days. Once you receive your residence permit, you must get a Saudi licence which is valid for three years and can sometimes be obtained within three days. To get it you will need to present your valid national licence, extra photographs, passport, and proof of your blood group. You will also be asked to undergo a medical checkup and eye test. Women are not allowed to drive except in the ARAMCO compound and so must rely on taxis or husbands. Families often share the cost of a driver.

Insurance coverage is not compulsory, but is highly recommended in case of accident and injury to third parties. Injured victims of traffic accidents are always awarded compensation from the driver of the other vehicle, regardless of fault. Inability to pay may well result in a prison sentence. For insurance claims, you need a police report to ascertain the fault of the parties. If you are involved in an accident, call the police and wait with your car for them to arrive.

Always have your driver's licence, car registration and other documentation with you, as well as a fire extinguisher and warning triangle. The police carry out regular spot checks. If they confiscate your licence they should give you a receipt for it.

Driving is on the right. At intersections, the car coming from the right has priority. Traffic signs conform to international designs and symbols. There is a general speed limit in the towns of 40 km. (25 miles) per hour, but there are no signs to indicate this and speeding is common. However, traffic infringements such as illegal U-turns or running stoplights are punished by fines and even a few days in jail.

Fluid measures

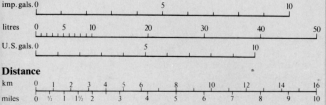

Distance

driving licence   **rúkhsit sawáaga**
insurance policy   **buléesit ta'méen**

Fill the tank, please.   **abéeha min fádlak**
I've had a breakdown.   **ta'áttalat sayyáaratee**
There's been an accident.   **fee háadithah**

113

E **ELECTRIC CURRENT.** It's both 220V and 110V AC, 60 cycles, in Riyadh, Jeddah and Dhahran, but other areas vary so it's always better to ask. Light bulbs have either the bayonet or screw fittings, and plugs are usually the continental round 2-pin type.

It's important to note that electric lines may not be earthed in Saudi Arabia so do not handle plugs with wet hands and make sure your children and servants understand the dangers of electricity.

There are occasional powercuts, and at such times it's best to unplug most electrical appliances as the sudden surge of power when the supply is reconnected can sometimes damage your equipment.

EMBASSIES and CONSULATES

Australia: P.O. Box 876, 59 Al Amir A. Al Faisal Street, Al Hamra, Ruwais, Jeddah; tel. 665 1303

Canada: P.O. Box 5050, 6th floor, Queen's Building, Commercial Centre, King Abdul Aziz Street, Jeddah; tel. 643 4597

United Kingdom: P.O. Box 393, Ha'il Street, Jeddah; tel. 660 4430

U.S.A.: P.O. Box 149, Palestine Road, Ruwais, Jeddah; tel. 667 0080

EMERGENCIES. Hotel staff and local police can always be called upon, but here are some useful numbers:

Accidents	993
Ambulance	997
Fire	998
Police	999

ENTRY FORMALITIES and CUSTOMS CONTROLS

Visas. Citizens of Bahrain, Kuwait, Oman, Qatar and the United Arab Emirates do not require entry visas. All other citizens require a valid visa. No tourist visas are given.

To obtain a visa, you will be asked to produce a passport valid for at least six months, photographs and sometimes a certificate or other evidence of religion. It is wise to take several extra photographs with you to Saudi Arabia and keep some proof of your religion with you in case it is necessary. Judaism and atheism are not acceptable.

Business visas may be granted for a 15-day trip (sometimes longer). Application should be made to the relevant Saudi embassy at least two weeks before departure. You will need to show the original of a letter from your Saudi sponsor confirming his invitation and giving the reasons for your visit.

Transit visas, allocated to people passing through the country, are only valid for one or two days. An onward ticket must be shown when applying. If you are merely in Saudi Arabia for a stopover of a few hours you do not need a visa, but you are restricted to the airport.

Work visa. If you are going to Saudi Arabia to work you will first need an entry visa. This is issued on presentation of a letter from your employer and sponsor and a copy of your contract. You are also required to produce documents issued by the Ministry of Foreign Affairs in Saudi Arabia which authorizes the issue of work permits to foreigners on the basis of an application by the employer.

Pilgrimage visas. Unlike other visas, the pilgrimage visa does not always require a passport and is issued solely to Muslims travelling to Saudi Arabia for the Hajj. There is no charge.

Visitor's visas. Wives and children under 18 who wish to visit a resident in Saudi Arabia should obtain a letter from the resident's employer. Children should also have a letter from their head teacher.

Before leaving the country, don't forget to obtain an exit visa, if you are leaving permanently, or a re-entry visa if you plan to return. This may take several days—longer during Ramadan and the Hajj season. All visiting businessmen as well as foreign residents must show their passports to the airline or travel agent at least 24 hours prior to departure.

Customs controls are strict, and luggage will be thoroughly inspected on arrival. Alcohol, pork products, narcotics and weapons, as well as pornographic films, photos and literature are all forbidden inside Saudi Arabia. Items such as cameras and typewriters may be subject to a duty, but this is refunded if the articles are re-exported within three months. Camera film should be in unopened packages. Sleeping pills, tranquillizers and stimulants are considered narcotics, and contraceptives may be confiscated, although they are available in pharmacies in Saudi Arabia. If you need to bring important medicines with you into the country, it's a good idea to have a copy of the prescription to accompany them. Archaeological artefacts and certain antiques may not be exported. Reasonable quantities of cigarettes, cigars and tobacco are allowed in duty free. There are no limits on the import or export of foreign currency.

Health regulations. Controls are made at each point of entry. You will be asked to present a certificate of vaccination against smallpox and cholera, and also yellow fever if arriving from a country where the disease is endemic. It is advisable to have inoculations against typhoid,

E tetanus, polio and possibly hepatitis, depending on general health and length of stay.

It is extremely important to check with the Saudi embassy on visa requirements and health regulations, as they are quite complicated and frequently subject to revision. Allow plenty of time for collecting the necessary documentation and having inoculations.

G **GUIDES and INTERPRETERS** *(daléel wa mutárjim)**. The services of guides and interpreters can be arranged through your hotel. Those performing the Hajj are allotted on arrival an official guide *(mutáw-wif)*, who will arrange transport and accommodation and lead the rites.

We'd like an English-speaking guide.	**nuréed daléel yatakállam ingléezee**
I'd like an English interpreter.	**uréed turjmáan ingléezee**

HAIRDRESSERS *(halláag)**. For men these can be found in all the large hotels. There are no public hairdressers for women, but private arrangements exist where there are large foreign communities.

H **HEALTH and MEDICAL CARE.** Make sure you have adequate insurance to cover accident, illness and hospitalization.

The climate is conducive to good health, and problems tend to be minor. The worst enemies are dehydration and heatstroke, but these can be avoided by increasing salt and fluid intake and wearing a hat whenever in the sun. Beware of excessive sunbathing until you are acclimatized. Contact lenses may be a problem in the dry, dusty conditions and you should bring your own wetting solution with you. Wash fruit and vegetables in a sterilizing agent and only buy very fresh local meat and fish.

Malaria tablets should be taken when travelling outside the main towns, particularly in the south. You must begin the treatment *before* your trip, and continue for a specified time after leaving the affected area.

Bilharzia (schistosomiasis) is a possible threat which might take the joy out of bathing in springs and lakes. Transmitted by a parasite whose intermediate host is a freshwater snail, this infection causes blood-stained urine and diarrhoea.

Facilities in the new hospitals are among the most modern in the world and many doctors have been trained in the West and consequently speak English. You are advised to find your own doctor and

116

dentist as soon as possible on arrival, as some hospitals will not admit expatriates except under emergency or for specialist care. Some foreign companies have their own private clinics for employees.

Pharmacies abound and hold extensive stocks of drugs and health-care products. Prescriptions for the medicines you will need should bear the generic as well as the brand name, which may be different.

In an emergency:

The Shumaisi Hospital, Riyadh, tel. 435 1900

Jeddah Medical Centre, tel. 669 0837; 651 5935

Get a doctor, quickly.	**jeeb tabéeb bi súr'a**
Where's the nearest (all-night) pharmacy?	**wayn ágrab saydaléeya (maftóoha bil-láyl)**
I have a pain here.	**yoojá'nee húnaa**
ambulance	**sayyáarat is'áaf**
hospital	**mustáshfaa**

HOTELS *(fúndug)**. International hotels of a high standard can be found in the major cities and the number is constantly increasing. Many offer additional office facilities for businessmen. A 15% service charge is added to bills, and there is a tax of 75% on all telephone calls and 40% on telex charges. Book well in advance and be sure to confirm your reservation, especially at holiday times. If you have any queries or complaints, contact the Ministry of Commerce (Hotels Department),

Riyadh tel. 401 2229; Jeddah tel. 642 3400.

HOURS. Friday is the Muslim day of rest. Thursday and Friday represent the weekend in Saudi Arabia, but you will find that most private organizations work during part of Thursday.

Muslims pray five times a day—at dawn *(fajr)*, at midday *(dhuhr)*, mid-afternoon *(asr)*, early evening 6–7 p.m. *(maghrib)*, late evening 7–8 p.m. *(isha)*. Shops close three times during the day for half an hour of prayer, and work in offices is interrupted, too. Check *Arab News* or *Saudi Gazette* for details of *salat* (prayer) times. During Ramadan, shops are closed for most of the day, opening only at sunset, sometimes until 2 a.m.

Shops. Hours for shops, supermarkets and souks vary slightly, but they are normally from 9 a.m.–12 p.m. and 4–9 p.m., Saturday to Thursday. Most shops in the souks stay open on Fridays.

H **Banks** do business from 8 a.m.–12 p.m. and approximately between 4.30 p.m. and 6.30 p.m., Saturday to Wednesday, and 8.30–11.30 a.m. on Thursday.

Post offices. A rough guide would be 7 a.m.–2 p.m. and 4–8 p.m., Saturday to Wednesday. Some post offices are open 24 hours a day.

Offices. Most government departments work from 7.30 a.m.–2.30 p.m., Saturday to Wednesday, and occasionally on Thursdays till noon. Commercial offices mainly work 8 a.m.–1 p.m. and 5–8 p.m.

Museums. Mostly open morning and afternoon every day except Friday, but hours vary and special times are reserved for men and women to visit separately. The same is true for the zoo in Riyadh.

L **LANGUAGE.** Arabic is the official language. Many Saudis have been educated in the West and so English is the *lingua franca* in business circles. But all documents are printed first in Arabic, and all foreign companies must correspond with the government in the official language.

If you take the trouble to learn some Arabic, it will be greatly appreciated and enhance your experience of the country. There are some letters which may cause problems to the English-speaker who is not accustomed to making the sounds. Here are some hints on how to pronounce them:

kh	like **ch** in Scottish lo**ch**
dh	like **th** in **th**en
'a	similar to a glottal stop
gh	like a gargled 'g' (or the Parisian rolling of **r** in "rue")
g	a deep-throated **k**, frequently pronounced as a 'g'

The Berlitz phrase book ARABIC FOR TRAVELLERS covers most situations you are likely to encounter in Saudi Arabia.

Do you speak English?	**tatakállam ingléezee**
I don't speak Arabic.	**ma atakállam arabée**
I don't understand.	**ma áfham**

LAUNDRY and DRY-CLEANING *(ghaséel, tanzéef)*. Laundry and dry-cleaning shops can be found in most cities but the most reliable service is offered by hotels.

LIVING IN SAUDI ARABIA. Foreigners living and working in Saudi Arabia need to have a residence permit, a white card with photograph attached, which is called the *iqama*. Temporary visas, such as business or visit visas may not normally be converted into residence visas without the applicant leaving the Kingdom.

Foreigners intending to work in Saudi Arabia need a work visa for entry to the country. The employer or sponsor in Saudi Arabia makes an application to the Ministry of the Interior, which confirms its approval to the Ministry of Foreign Affairs, which in turn notifies the Saudi Embassy abroad. The work visa is valid for three months, but the employer should apply for a residence permit on his employee's behalf within three days of the latter's arrival in Saudi Arabia. Once issued, the residence permit is normally valid for two years. But each time the employee leaves the country he must get a re-entry visa in order to return. When leaving for good, he must obtain an exit visa. Carry your *iqama* with you at all times as identification and evidence of your residence permit.

If you plan to work in Saudi Arabia, make sure that your contract is clear and unambiguous. Check on who is paying for holidays, expenses, family allowances, etc. Only certain categories of foreigners —mainly professional—are allowed to bring their families with them to Saudi Arabia. If your family is coming with you, they will need visas, too. You will not be allowed to bring any pets with you.

Housing. Foreigners are not generally allowed to own land, so your house will probably be leased. It will be a villa, an apartment or a unit in a housing compound. If your company does not provide accommodation for you and you have to arrange your own, your housing may be negotiated for you by an estate agent. You must be sure to obtain translations of all documents pertaining to the transaction and before signing, try to inspect the house yourself or at least ascertain whether it is habitable and whether all the specified utilities are there. You should familiarize yourself with landlord and tenant responsibilities. For instance, the tenant has to pay for any damage to the house caused by fire, a strong argument in favour of insurance, while the landlord is bound to carry out structural repairs. Rent is usually payable one or two years in advance. Find out if it includes the cost of utilities. Watch out for clauses which expect you to leave expensive fixtures and fittings such as air-conditioners in the house when you leave. The estate agent will receive commission for arranging the transaction.

Servants. If you decide to employ servants, you must check that they have a valid work permit. Employing illegal workers may result in a prison sentence.

Schools. Non-Muslim children attend fee-paying co-ed schools which are suitable up to the age of 12 or so. But they are expensive and

L teenage children are better off going to school in Bahrain, Egypt or your home country. The school year is from September to June. Enrol your child early. No school uniform is necessary. There are a number of private playgroups for preschool-age children, mainly run by expatriate wives. Some companies have schools for the children of their employees, and other families educate their children through correspondence courses. If your children are at school abroad, remember that they will need visas to enter Saudi Arabia to visit you in their holidays.

LOST PROPERTY. By and large, if you leave anything in a hotel or restaurant, you will be fairly certain of finding it again. Staff are very obliging and will help you to trace something left on a bus or train. Otherwise, ask the police, and in the case of a lost passport, contact your embassy.

I have lost my wallet/handbag/ passport.	**dayyáat máhfidhatee / shántat yádee / basbóoree**

M MONEY MATTERS

Currency. Saudi Arabia's unit of currency is the *riyal,* divided into 100 *halalah.* Notes come in denominations of 1, 5, 10, 50, 100 and 500 riyal, and coins in 5, 10, 25 and 50 halalah. Inflation has made the coins almost worthless but they are useful for public telephones, so hang onto them.

Banks and currency exchange. There are no restrictions on currency exchange. You can change money at banks (see under HOURS) and hotels, though the latter will give a less favourable rate. Money changers can be found at international airports and near the souks. As well as dealing in cash, they issue personal cheques, traveller's cheques and bank drafts. Some have accounts worldwide and can arrange complicated transactions. Their hours vary according to prayer times, but are approximately 9 a.m.–noon and 4–8 p.m. An array of foreign banknotes advertises this service.

Credit cards and traveller's cheques. Major credit cards are accepted at most large hotels, some restaurants and the bigger stores. Most airline offices also accept them. But cash is by far the preferred medium for transactions of all kinds. Don't make a trip to the souk without cash. Traveller's cheques can be bought at the airport. Always take your passport with you if you intend to change money, pay with a traveller's cheque or use your credit card.

I want to change some pounds/dollars.	wúdee ásrif juneiháat/ dóolaaraat
Do you accept traveller's cheques?	tigbal sheekáat siyáaheeya
Can I pay with this credit card?	múmkin ádfa' máa kaart ad-dimáana háadha

NEWSPAPERS and MAGAZINES *(jaréeda wa majálla)**. Almost every hotel has a kiosk selling Saudi and international papers. The English-language dailies are the *Saudi Gazette* and *Arab News. Saudi Business* is a weekly aimed at businessmen.

| Do you have any English-language newspapers? | 'indekum jaráayid ingléezeeya |

PHOTOGRAPHY. Photography is a sensitive subject in Saudi Arabia, although the Saudis are more relaxed than they used to be on such matters. The golden rule is to ask first and to be discreet. Permission from the Ministry of Information may be needed. People are more tolerant in the big cities and photography is expressly permitted in Dir'iyah. It is illegal to photograph certain military or government establishments such as airports, and taboo to take pictures of women.

Film is readily available and quickly processed. Cameras can be bought at reasonable prices. They should be cleaned frequently because of the dust and protected from the sun. A polarizing filter can help to bring out full colours.

I'd like a film for this camera.	uréed li háadhihil kamera
black and white film	film áswad wa ábyad
colour prints	súwar bil alwáan
colour slides	slayd bil alwáan
How long will it take to develop this film?	mátaa tígdar tuhammíd lee háadhal film
May I take your picture?	múmkin áakhud sóoratak

POLICE. Police may be recognized by their white hats and khaki uniforms. Police emergency tel. 999.

| Where's the nearest police station? | wayn ágrab márkaz lish-shúrta |
| Please can you help me. | saa'ídnee min fádlak |

P **PUBLIC HOLIDAYS.** There are no secular public holidays. Business activity is severely restricted during Ramadan and stops altogether for three days during Id al Fitr, the breaking of the fast at the end of Ramadan. This period is customarily a 10-day holiday for ministries and other government offices. The other important feast day, when business ceases for about four days, is the Id al Adha on the tenth of Dhu al Hijjah, the month of pilgrimage. Again this period is a 10-day holiday for government offices. Also observed is 1st Muharram, the new year, and by many the 10th Muharram as well.

Visiting businessmen would do well to avoid the period of Ramadan and the Hajj season. Although business goes on during Ramadan, working hours are severely shortened; during the Hajj the needs of the Muslim pilgrims are given priority over business dealings.

R **RADIO and TV.** Radio and television programmes mostly cater for the tastes of the local people, so that non-Arabic speakers have a limited choice. There are news bulletins, cartoons and other special features in English on Saudi television, but in the Eastern Province ARAMCO TV offers a wider selection of familiar programmes for expatriates, and videocassettes with the latest films are available.

The BBC World Service and Voice of America can be reached on shortwave, and both Radio Jeddah and Radio Riyadh carry programmes in English and French on AM and FM frequencies. ARAMCO has four FM stations offering news and all kinds of music. For details, consult *Arab News.*

RELIGIOUS SERVICES. No religious practices apart from those of the Muslim faith are permitted in Saudi Arabia.

T **TIME DIFFERENCES.** GMT + 3 hours is recognized by law all year round, but traditional Arabic time may still be found. This is how it works: timepieces are set to 12 at the local time of sunset when the new day begins. Thus ten o'clock is four o'clock in the afternoon, Western time, two hours before sunset and the end of the day.

	New York	London	**Riyadh**	Sydney	Auckland
January	4 a.m.	9 a.m.	**noon**	8 p.m.	10 p.m.
July	5 a.m.	10 a.m.	**noon**	7 p.m.	9 p.m.

122 What time is it, please? **kam as-sáa'a**

TIPPING. Though not obligatory, tipping is customary and will smooth your path considerably. A refusal should be respected. Round off bills and give the odd coin whenever it seems appropriate. There is no need to tip taxi drivers. For other cases, here are some indications:

Hairdresser	10%
Houseboy per week	SR 5–10
Porter, per bag	SR 2
Tour guide	discuss with hotel services first
Waiter	15% of bill unless service charge already indicated on bill

TOILETS *(tawáalet).* Public toilets are few and far between. Naturally you will find one at a café and in hotel lobbies. Sometimes you will find one near a mosque.

Where are the toilets, please?   **wayn at-tawáalet min fádlak**

TRANSPORT*

Air. Internal flights are run by SAUDIA and heavily subsidized, therefore cheap. Since Saudi Arabia is such an enormous country this is a popular method of getting around and flights are full. The route most commonly used by foreigners is Jeddah/Riyadh/Dhahran, flown by the Arabian Express which leaves hourly. Only first-class tickets can be reserved. All other tickets are distributed on a first-come, first-served basis the day before the intended flight. Demand frequently outstrips the available seats. Ask at the SAUDIA office in your hotel for advice on procedures. Women are not supposed to travel alone by air, but must have a male relative accompanying them.

Bus. Saudi Arabian Public Transport Company (SAPTCO) runs an efficient public bus service in most of the major cities. Vehicles have a special section for women at the back with a separate entrance. Routes are published in Saudi daily newspapers, and complete timetables are available from SAPTCO. Jitneys are a privately-owned form of bus service, usually crowded but handy. Some of the principal hotels in Jeddah offer their guests a complimentary bus service to and from the airport.

T

Intercity bus services run between Jeddah, Mecca, Medina and Ta'if, as well as the towns in the Eastern Province. Buses are air-conditioned and have toilets.

Taxi. All kinds of vehicles ply the main thoroughfares, picking up passengers for a flat fee and dropping them off where they want along the route. If you try one, remember to call out *nazil* when you want to get off. However, it is best to use the official yellow taxis, which may or may not have meters. Official prices at airports are not often respected but will give you an idea of the going rate. Find out from friends what the standard fare is for a short distance (2 km. or so) and for a long distance within a city. Fix a price before getting in. This is your chance to practise your Arabic as well as your bargaining skills. If you are reluctant to haggle, try the limousines. Fares are fixed and the cars are roomy and air-conditioned. There are taxis with English-speaking drivers provided by the main hotels. Private cars also act as taxis and are frequently driven by students who often willingly act as guides and interpreters. Women are advised not to take taxis alone.

Train. A passenger train runs daily from Riyadh to Dammam. The journey takes about 7 hours with a stop at Hufuf and elsewhere. It is air-conditioned (you will probably need a jacket). Tickets should be bought the day before, and you will need to show your passport. Women should not travel unaccompanied.

Where's the bus for ...?	**wayn máwgif al baas li**
Taxi!	**taxi**
What's the fare to?	**kam al újra li**
That's too much.	**kithéer jíddan**
Take me to ...	**wadéenee li**

W

WATER. Water from the tap is chlorinated and therefore drinkable, but the high mineral content may upset the stomach and even cause serious health problems in the long term. It is better to stick to bottled mineral water at all times.

Is this drinking water?	**hal háadha maay lish-shúrb**

124

SOME USEFUL EXPRESSIONS

Yes/No.	ná'am/laa
Please (m/f).	min fádlak/min fádlik
Thank you.	shúkran
Don't mention it.	áfwan
where/when/how	wayn/mátaa/kayf
how long will it take	kam yákhud waqt
how far	kam al-masáafah
yesterday/today/tomorrow	ams/alyáwm/báakir (búkrah)
day/week/month/year	yawm/usbóo'ah/shahr/sánah
morning/afternoon/	sabáah/b'ád adh-dúhr/
evening/night	másaa/layl
left/right	yasáar/yaméen
big/small	kabéer/saghéer
cheap/expensive	rakhées/gháalee
old/new	qadéem/jadéed
here/there	húnaa/hunáak
open/closed	maftóoh/musákkar
early/late	mubákkir/muta'ákhir
easy/difficult	sahl/sá'ab
good/bad	táyyib/ma táyyib
	zayn/ma zayn
stop/go	owgaf/rooh
Mr./Mrs.	sáyyid/sáyyidah
Peace be upon you.	as-saláam aláykum
(reply) And on you be peace.	wa aláykum as-saláam
How are you?	kayf háalak
(reply) I'm fine, praise God.	bikhayr, al-hámdu lilláh
Good morning. (until midday)	sabáah al-khayr
(reply)	sabáah an-noor
Good evening.	fee amáan illáh
Goodbye.	ma'a saláamah
Hello.	áhlan wa śahlan (sometimes just áhlan)
Sorry/Excuse me.	ana muta'ássif
I'd like...	uréed/ábghaa
How much?	kam háadha/bi kam

NUMBERS

1	**waáhid (m) waáhidah (f)**	20	**'ishréen**
2	**ithnáyn**	30	**thalaathéen**
3	**thaláathah**	40	**arba'éen**
4	**árba'ah**	50	**khamséen**
5	**khámsah**	60	**sittéen**
6	**síttah**	70	**saba'éen**
7	**sáb'ah**	80	**thamaanéen**
8	**thamáanyah**	90	**tis'éen**
9	**tís'ah**	100	**míyah**
10	**'áshrah**	200	**miyatáyn**
11	**ihdá'sh**	300	**thaláath míyah**
12	**ithná'sh**	400	**arba' míyah**
13	**thalaata'sh**	500	**khams míyah**
14	**'arba'atá'sh**	600	**sitt míyah**
15	**khamstá'sh**	700	**saba' míyah**
16	**sittá'sh**	800	**thamáan míyah**
17	**saba'tá'sh**	900	**tisa' míyah**
18	**thamaantá'sh**	1000	**alf**
19	**tis'tá'sh**		

DAYS OF THE WEEK

Sunday	– **yawm al-áhad**	Wednesday	– **yawm al-árba'ah**
Monday	– **yawm al-ithnáyn**	Thursday	– **yawm al-khamées**
Tuesday	– **yawm ath-thaláa-thah**	Friday	– **yawm al-júma'a**
		Saturday	– **yawm as-sábt**

MONTHS

January	– **yanáa'ir**	July	– **yóolyoo**
February	– **fibráa'ir**	August	– **aaghústus**
March	– **máaris**	September	– **sabtámbir**
April	– **abréel**	October	– **uktóobir**
May	– **máayoo**	November	– **noofámbir**
June	– **yóonyoo**	December	– **deesámbir**

Index

An asterisk (*) next to a page number indicates a map reference. Where there is more than one set of page references, the one in bold type refers to the main entry. For index to Practical Information, see p. 109.

INDEX

128